AS Film Studies
UNIT 2

D1342418

Unit FS2: Producers and Audiences

Tanya Jones and Tony Dyson

Philip Allan Updates
Market Place
Deddington
Oxfordshire
OX15 0SE

Tel: 01869 338652
Fax: 01869 337590
e-mail: sales@philipallan.co.uk
www.philipallan.co.uk

© Philip Allan Updates 2004

ISBN 0 86003 926 9

All rights reserved; no part of this publication may be reproduced, stored
in a retrieval system, or transmitted, in any form or by any means, electronic,
mechanical, photocopying, recording or otherwise without either the prior
written permission of Philip Allan Updates or a licence permitting restricted
copying in the United Kingdom issued by the Copyright Licensing Agency Ltd,
90 Tottenham Court Road, London W1P 9HE.

This guide has been written specifically to support students preparing for the
WJEC Film Studies Unit 2 examination. The content has been neither approved
nor endorsed by WJEC and remains the sole responsibility of the authors.

Printed by Information Press, Eynsham, Oxford

Contents

Introduction

■ ■ ■

Content Guidance

■ ■ ■

Questions and Answers

Introduction

About this guide

This guide is for students following the Welsh Joint Education Committee AS Film Studies course. It deals with **Unit FS2: Producers and Audiences**. This unit is designed to give you a good understanding of the film industry and of film consumption. There are three sections to this guide.

- **Introduction** — this provides advice on how to use the guide, an explanation of the skills required for the unit, an outline of the exam structure and guidance on study skills.
- **Content Guidance** — this outlines the areas you need to focus on for the unit. It is designed to help you structure your revision and make you aware of the content needed.
- **Questions and Answers** — this provides questions similar to those in sections A and B of Unit 2. It includes examples of A-grade and C-grade answers. Examiner's comments follow each one; these explain how the marks are awarded.

How to use the guide

To get the maximum possible benefit from this guide, use it systematically. Make sure you read through the whole of the Introduction carefully. When you have a thorough overview of the skills needed for this unit and the format of the exam, you should move on to the next section.

The Content Guidance section aims to lead you through the essential content areas and highlight particular skills and theories. It would be extremely useful for you to make notes on your own examples and experiences as you read through the content areas. You have essential experience as a consumer of cinema and the exam board encourages the addition of points that reflect your own experience.

When you have completed your study of content, you should then move on to look at the Questions and Answers section. Here you will find examples of types of exam question. For each of the questions, A-grade and C-grade answers have been provided, to illustrate what it takes to achieve a high grade. Take note of the structure of the A-grade answers, as well as the information they contain. Make sure that you read the examiner's comments on each answer too, noting the features of the answers that are praised and the possible pitfalls.

The Unit 2 specification

This unit focuses on the film industry and film consumption. You need a good understanding of the film business and the issues involved in how audiences respond to film. You were introduced to Hollywood films in Unit 1 through your macro-analysis essay. This knowledge can be used within your answers in the Unit 2 exam.

Unit 2 requires a good understanding of all aspects of the film industry, from film financing to production, distribution and exhibition. You will need to show your knowledge of:
- how films move from an initial concept to the point where filming commences
- how films are marketed
- the process of getting a finished film into the cinema

The role of stars in the creation of and publicity for a film is also an area you need to investigate, as is the impact of new technologies on the film industry. Issues concerning film audiences are an essential area of study. You need to exhibit clear knowledge of which technologies we use to consume films and of the impact of audience opinion on the film industry. Bringing your own experience as a film consumer into the discussion is essential.

The full title of this unit is **Producers and Audiences: Hollywood and British Cinema**, so you need to focus on these two industries only. The changes in the Hollywood and British industries over the last decades and the differences in how these two industries are organised are important areas. The specification asks that you consider the film industry and film audiences as interacting entities. Try not to study these two areas in isolation, but as mutually informing topics for debate.

Skills required for this unit

For the Unit 2 exam you need to show:
- an understanding of how cinema functions as a business and how this business interacts with its audience
- a critical understanding of your own experience as a consumer, fan and critic of cinema

You need to express clearly your knowledge of all aspects of the film industry. You must discuss how film financing, production, distribution and exhibition function within the British and Hollywood systems, with accuracy, confidence and clarity. Don't just retell the information you have gathered. Discuss the differences between the Hollywood and British industries and evaluate whether the various sections of the film industry work together harmoniously. Make sure that you provide your own examples, as well as using those that you have been given. You want your answer to stand out to the examiner. Therefore, you need to distinguish it from other answers by the addition of different examples and references. When discussing the role of the audience within film production, offer concrete examples of the impact of audience response on a film or the means by which film producers gather audience opinion before releasing a film.

Ensure that when making your points you include specific references to films you have seen. Try to reflect on your behaviour and response when engaging with a particular film or type of film. Discussion of your expectation of certain genres, or the effect of pre-release publicity on your response to a film, is far more relevant than merely telling the examiner about your least and most favourite films.

The exam

Unit 2 is worth 30% of the AS marks and 15% of the whole A-level grade. The exam lasts for 90 minutes and you have to answer two questions. Each question is worth 25 marks. The balance of marks for each of the questions is equal, so you should spend an equal amount of time on each. You should allow 10 minutes for reading the exam paper thoroughly and spend 40 minutes answering each question.

The examination paper usually contains an extra section of resource material, which you should study carefully before selecting which questions to answer. There are four questions — two in Section A and two in Section B. You have to answer one question from each section. Section A is about audiences and Section B is about producers. Each section will give you the opportunity to exhibit your skills of analysis and debate. You may be given statistics to analyse — for example, on box-office receipts or film financing. You could be given posters to analyse that require you to discuss marketing and publicity, as well as audience expectations and responses. You might be asked to evaluate the role of a particular star in the marketing of a film. The questions in Unit 2 are problem-solving exercises. For example, if you are asked a question such as 'Who are the stars in contemporary cinema and why?', it is essential that you not only state *who* you think the stars are but *why* they are stars. Whatever you are faced with in the exam, if you have covered the key areas for this unit in your revision, you will be completely prepared.

Study skills and revision strategies

The golden rule of revision is not to leave it until just before your exam. You should begin to prepare for the exam from the outset of your AS course. If you organise your notes from the beginning, you will not have to waste time sifting through them close to the exam date. Always keep your notes in a folder or folders, with dividers indicating the topic in each section. For this unit, you should have a section for each of the topics covered in the Content Guidance part of this guide. Within each section, you should highlight key words or terms that you will need to refer to in the exam.

Your own experiences as a consumer, fan and critic of cinema will provide useful points of reference in your exam answers. As you check through each of the sections within the Unit 2 part of your folder, make sure that you have also included personal comments and investigations, and have noted any names, dates and statistics that might be useful. For example, if you have a section of notes discussing the critical and financial reception of a film you have seen, you should add comments concerning your own expectations of, and responses to, this film.

There are numerous sources that you can use to research your personal examples. The publication, author and date of these should also be noted. The *Internet Movie Database* (**www.imdb.com**) is one of many useful on-line sources. Film magazines, such as *Total Film, Sight and Sound, Empire* and *Premiere* can also provide helpful information. In addition, there are numerous film studies textbooks available.

Content revision will take up a significant proportion of your revision time. However, having a clear knowledge of terms and content is not the only area of preparation on which you should concentrate. The Unit 2 exam requires you to write answers within a limited time and so you need to practise writing under timed conditions. The section in this Introduction outlining the exam indicates that 40 minutes for each question would be appropriate. You should train yourself to be able to write comprehensive, well-structured answers within that time. You could use the Questions and Answers section of this guide to pick up tips on organising answers and then ask your teacher for old exam papers to practise under timed conditions.

If you begin the revision process early in your course, by rereading your notes and adding personal examples, then you will avoid having to rush your revision at a later date. Information that you understand thoroughly at the time you receive it will stick with you if you ask questions in class and reread your notes after lessons. If you do this, you will be able to approach your final revision in a more relaxed and confident manner.

Content
Guidance

This section summarises the main areas you need to focus on in your preparation for the Unit 2 exam. It outlines content information, key issues and useful terminology, and gives guidance on how to use your knowledge in answering exam questions. The notes you have made in class and the information given to you by your teacher should be used alongside the information given in this section. Your personal investigations from film textbooks, magazines, websites and other resources should also be added to notes you take from this section.

This section covers:

- **The Hollywood film industry, then and now**
- **Film finance**
- **Film production**
- **Film distribution and exhibition**
- **The British film industry, then and now**
- **Film consumption: the cinema audience**
- **The star system**
- **Film and new technologies**

Films that have an 18 certificate have been identified with an asterisk. Your teacher will advise you of the suitability of any 18-certified films for study purposes.

The Hollywood film industry, then and now

The structure of the Hollywood film industry has changed significantly over the last 75 years, as have the films produced. Your notes should cover all the issues that might come up in the exam and you should be able to discuss:

- the changes that have occurred in the Hollywood film industry
- the differences between the film industries in Hollywood and in Britain
- the types of film product that the contemporary Hollywood film industry produces

The studio system

The Hollywood studio system had its golden age between 1930 and 1948. During this period, films were made on a **production line** model, which often invited the criticism that the films produced were too formulaic and similar. Five companies dominated the film industry:

- Paramount
- Loew's (the parent company of MGM)
- Fox Film
- Warner Brothers
- RKO

Three smaller companies (Columbia, Universal and United Artists) existed in Hollywood, but did not own cinemas and needed to maintain a good relationship with the 'big five' to be sure of wide cinematic release.

Each studio was controlled by a powerful individual — a mogul — who oversaw all aspects of the studio's functioning. Darryl F. Zanuck was one of the most famous and he controlled the careers of many important stars. Betty Grable, a huge star during the Hollywood golden age, was one of Zanuck's most famous products.

Paramount had more than 1,000 theatres in its cinema chain and therefore had the biggest hold over film exhibition. Fox became 20th Century Fox in 1935 and from then on found financial success. RKO was the shortest lived of the studios and was the least profitable, despite producing films such as *Citizen Kane* in 1941. MGM was perhaps the most famous of the major studios. All of the five major companies were organised on a model of **vertical integration**. They each owned the means to produce, distribute and exhibit (show) their films and because of this they dominated the film industry in the 1930s and 1940s. These companies did not have to buy in the services of distributors or cinema owners and could keep all their profits under one roof.

However, the dominance of the five major studios did not last. At the end of the Second World War, a combination of social, economic and political forces brought the studio system to an end. Many Americans, after years of financial hardship and anxiety resulting from the war, moved to the suburbs in an attempt to create stress-free family lives. The movement out of the cities of vast numbers of people led to a decline in cinema attendance and box-office takings. Eventually, many of the big movie palaces were forced to close. The final end to the studio system came in 1948, with the Paramount decree, which was a Supreme Court ruling that forced the major companies to sell their cinemas. Effectively, the monopoly of the 'big five' was broken. The major studios did not collapse, but their particular version of vertical integration no longer existed, because they no longer owned all three main film production areas.

Hollywood today

The Hollywood of today is a different place. The studio system as it was in the 1930s and 1940s does not exist. Studios no longer make films, but film deals.

An independent individual, such as a producer or a sales agent, puts together a **package** that they then present to potential investors. The package consists of:
- a **treatment** for a film (longer than a synopsis, but not yet a full script)
- details of actors/actresses attached to the project
- details of the proposed director and locations

Film studios may be the investors to whom the 'package' is presented. If the studio likes the film, then it will agree to produce and finance it.

Today there are more than a dozen film studios in Los Angeles, including MGM, Warner Brothers, Sony Pictures Studios, Paramount, Universal, 20th Century Fox and DreamWorks. Four out of the 'big five' studios of the Hollywood golden age still exist.

Some studios have particular relationships with directors and give them 'first options' on film ideas. For example, Steven Spielberg has a first option agreement with DreamWorks.

In the year 2001–02, Warner Brothers (founded in 1923) produced the first two Harry Potter films, *The Lord of the Rings* parts 1 and 2, *Scooby-Doo* and the Austin Powers *Goldmember* instalment. Its output is enormous. Moreover, Warner Brothers owns the Warner Brothers cinema chain, and can therefore show its own films in its own cinemas. Perhaps vertical integration did not completely cease to exist at the end of the studio era.

Blockbusters and high-concept films

For your study of Hollywood film products, you could begin by listing prominent Hollywood films in the marketplace today and then analyse them for any consistent

features. The terms **blockbuster** and **high-concept film** are often used to describe Hollywood films and you need to be sure that you understand these terms thoroughly. Often used interchangeably, blockbusters and high-concept films share a range of characteristics, which are outlined below.

Storyline

The basic storyline of the film is simple and universally recognisable

In order for a film to succeed outside an English-speaking market, it must be based on a story type that has universal appeal. Many films make most of their profits from international sales, either at the box office or on VHS and DVD. They therefore need to be understood outside the US market. Simple storylines succeed best. Love stories, often with tragic endings, have been universally popular from Shakespeare's time (e.g. *Romeo and Juliet*) to the present day. *Titanic* merged a well-known historical event with a universally popular story of love and loss, gaining huge financial rewards for its producers. The *Star Wars* films, at core, are about the struggle between good and evil, and as such are accessible to any audience.

Characters

The characters are simple to understand

The characters in blockbusters/high-concept films do not have complicated psychological conditions or motivations. They are not stereotypes either, but individuals with whom the viewer can identify and understand. For example, in the *Jurassic Park* films, the function of the human characters is to provide responses to the main characters of the film — the dinosaurs. Peter Parker in *Spider-Man* is a simple young man who becomes a superhero and fights evil and injustice. You could argue that Peter Parker/Spider-Man is only as engaging as the special effects used to create the character. Characters who do not have this universal appeal and who are either overly complex, or attached too specifically to a particular culture, do not translate well into the foreign market.

Selling

The film is sold on its 'look'

Much of the cost of blockbusters and high-concept films goes on special effects and high production values. The film looks slick and expensive. As such, the set pieces of a film and its dramatic new special effects are a perfect marketing focus for the producer. Viewers do not expect subtlety of characterisation or complexity of plot from a blockbuster, but they do expect a spectacular piece of entertainment. Look at the trailers for forthcoming films. You will be able to identify blockbusters from the content of the trailer. For example, the *Mission: Impossible* trailers give a clear indication that spectacular set action pieces form a significant part of the films. The feat of reproducing a realistic ocean liner was a key element of the advertising campaign for *Titanic*.

Profits

The film is only the beginning...

The huge initial investment needed to produce blockbusters/high-concept films is not quite the gamble it might initially seem. Advertising budgets are extremely high and many films do not break even at the box office. However, for a film that has universal appeal, the potential profit from the sale of satellite and terrestrial television rights, VHS/DVD sales and merchandising is enormous. From *Star Wars* onwards, there has been a vast market for collectables and other types of film merchandise. Consider all the toys, clothes, games and accessories available when a blockbuster is released; it is clear how the producers make their profits from these high-concept films.

Tip If you have read through this section carefully and have made notes on your own Hollywood film examples, then you will be prepared for exam questions on the Hollywood film industry. Remember, you will never be asked merely to describe what has changed since the time of the studio system. You have to be able to discuss particular areas. You might be asked why the studio system was so successful, or why Hollywood still seems to dominate world markets, or what the pros and cons are of a vertically integrated system. All of the answers are discussed above, but you should always read content information with a challenging mind — a mind that considers the impact of events on the industry and the consumer.

By using this section outlining the structure of the Hollywood system and the later section describing the British film industry, you should be able to compile a list of similarities and differences. Look for structural and financial differences, as well as those that exist between the products released.

> **Key words**

> production line model; vertical integration; the package; treatment; blockbuster/high-concept film

Film finance

Film is a medium in which creativity and business are forced to meet. The film industry is designed to make money through entertaining an audience. The US film industry is one of the USA's largest exporters. Financing film productions might seem to be a glamorous activity, but investing in a film is no guarantee of financial success. There is no such thing as a safe bet, because each film is to some extent a one-off prototype. (However, Hollywood studios try to reduce the high risks of film production by recombining/repackaging previously successful elements.) Hollywood takes risks on a scale few other industries would dare to contemplate.

> Of every ten films made in Hollywood, six will lose money from exhibition in cinemas, one break even, one make a little money, one make good money and one be such a successful blockbuster that it pays for all the others.
>
> (Armyan Bernstein, producer of *Air Force One* and other films)

For the Hollywood studios, a successful movie is a profitable movie. It is a commercial enterprise.

> It's not called show show, it's called show business. Somebody's going to invest capital with you in order to bring other people from your 'Eureka!' — your vision of your idea — into their 'Wow!' — the audience seeing it. You've got to put those two pieces together. You're not making this film for yourself in a dark screening room, you're making this film for a commercial audience. If that's not your intention, then maybe you should be in another business, maybe you should be a poet or something.
>
> (Peter Guber, producer of *Batman* and other films)

Filmmaking involves high overhead costs to finance the three main stages a film goes through before it is released to an audience:

- production
- distribution
- exhibition

Therefore, those who put up the money — investors, financiers, distributors and exhibitors — might have a significant influence over the film at certain key stages. When you are considering your own case-study films, make sure that you distinguish between the money spent on each of the three stages of production. Ask yourself what the balance is between the money spent on each of the three stages.

The producer

The producer has a variety of roles. The chief job is not just raising finance, but raising confidence in the initial idea. The idea — the first stage in the life of a film — may originate from a writer, a director or a producer and could be a book, a play, a television series, a comic strip, a computer game or another film. All of these can be pillaged in the quest for film fodder. Adaptations make up 50% of Hollywood's output. Using books as source material gives a film the benefit of an existing story plus brand recognition, as with *Harry Potter* and *The Lord of the Rings*, and brings a ready-made audience. Such is the competition to secure bestsellers that Warner Brothers is reported to have paid J.K. Rowling an undisclosed seven-figure sum for the rights to the *Harry Potter* novels.

The package

The package put together by a producer and presented to potential investors, financiers and distributors must include the following key elements and selling points:

- a **script treatment** — detailed storylines, possible stars and locations. This runs from 1 to 10 or more pages and is more than a synopsis. The script itself will need development money, which is high-risk because the film might never be made
- generic characteristics — whether the film belongs to a currently fashionable genre or a 'hybrid' genre similar to other recent films that have made money

- a proposed budget
- a storyboard of some key scenes
- the director and/or writer — an established name with a proven track record (someone whom the target audience might recognise and who has been responsible for other successful films) will reassure investors
- the potential cast being considered for the film. Britain has very few 'bankable' stars who can hold a movie together, unless they have been to Hollywood, featured successfully and then returned to British film
- other key creative personnel — the cinematographer, art director, editor and special effects team
- any possible marketing spin-offs — to give the film more publicity and profitability

The pitch

The **pitch** is the term used for the presentation of the package by the producer to a potential financial backer. If the pitch is for a large-budget film to a major studio, the most popular technique is to introduce the story by describing it as a hybrid of a pair of hit movies. For example, *RoboCop* is *Terminator* meets *Dirty Harry**. Pitches tend to be based on a straightforward and easily understood plot, with character and narrative reduced and simplified to a minimum. They are designed to present ideas that are high-concept.

High-concept films

High-concept films are a response by Hollywood studios to the high risks of film production. They may involve:
- repackaging previously successful elements, such as big name stars and/or directors
- remaking past hits in the form of either sequels (extending the franchise) or variations on currently fashionable genres. This often means mixing genres — such as combining action-adventure with comedy, romance, science fiction and so on.

Many critics argue that the intention is to make audiences become engaged with the 'surface' features of visual set pieces at the expense of coherent narrative development or characterisation. Whole scenes (especially action set pieces such as fights and chases) are linked only loosely to a narrative based on cause and effect and to characters who are psychologically well-motivated and convincingly developed. *Mission: Impossible* and *Tomb Raider* have been quoted as examples of this tendency. The action sequences built around amazing special effects, the most elaborately acrobatic fights and the longest car chase up to that date (17 minutes) were what impressed most audiences about *The Matrix Reloaded* — even if they never really became involved with the narrative or characters, or if they thought that the film became bogged down in the scenes between the action sequences, in which secondary characters indulged in rambling, inconsequential philosophising.

In high-concept movies, parts of the film can be easily transferred or adapted into other 'windows' of exhibition, such as a pop video for the soundtrack or a computer game. For example, the computer game *Enter the Matrix* was released in the same week as *The Matrix Reloaded* and was also expected to make a substantial profit.

Commitment to invest

Investors will only commit to a package when they have a clear presentation of the target audience and market(s) likely to be attracted by the selling points of the film. They need to be persuaded that a return on their investment is possible. Only then will they strike a deal with the producer, giving a project the 'green light', which means the studio agrees to fund the next stage, whether it be writing the screenplay or putting a finished screenplay into production.

Think of a film made within the last 2 years that you have seen recently. Why do you think investors funded it? Make a list of its 'selling points' — genre(s), stars, director, special effects and other aspects that might have attracted an audience.

Investors

There are various types of investor who are prepared to finance films.

Funding by studios

If a major studio is directly producing the film, it will usually finance it.

Many independent producers who develop ideas and raise the money for a movie also have a short-term production contract with a studio. In this sense, they are dependent producers rather than 'independent' ones, because they depend on the studio for funding. Studios usually insist on the right to approve the script, cast and budget of any film they finance.

There are **first-look contracts**, by which the producer agrees to give the studio the first opportunity to accept or reject the package before it is offered to any other studio. The studio covers the overhead costs and pays the producer a fee in advance of making the film, in return for a share of the profits.

An **exclusive contract** commits the producer to developing and producing all his or her projects for one studio.

In a **housekeeping deal**, the producer gets to develop the package using the studio's finances, giving them the first opportunity to accept or reject the film. If the studio accepts, it will finance the rest of the production, again in return for a share of the profits.

Funding for independent films

An independent film is a production developed and realised outside a major studio. Money might come from sources such as banks, investment companies, rich private investors and the government. It is more likely that the producers will try to pre-sell the film to distributors and sales agents, either for specific national markets or even for the worldwide rights. Selling the television, satellite and cable rights is another possibility.

The danger with allowing distributors and sales agents to become involved at an early stage of the project — in providing development money for example — is that they will demand more creative control. For example, Mick Jagger and Victoria Pearman, who run Jagged Films, could only raise the final part of the $8 million needed for their film based on the life of the Welsh poet Dylan Thomas by striking a deal with the Isle of Man Film Commission, on condition that half the film would be shot there instead of in Wales.

The Jagged Films deal was made at the Cannes Film Festival. Film festivals often function as trade fairs where production and distribution deals are struck. For example, the Sundance Film Festival held in Utah is a celebration of independent filmmaking, giving new cinematic talents a chance to shine by inviting them into competition and offering prizes. It is also a chance to pick up multi-million dollar Hollywood deals.

Bankability

There is a select group of stars who can guarantee a film's international success on the strength of their name alone. Bankability is the ability of a star's name to:
- raise money for a film
- attract support from major studios
- pull in cinema-goers at the box office

According to the last list compiled by the *Hollywood Reporter* (one of the trade bibles) in 2002, only three actors have a bankability rating of 100% — Julia Roberts, Tom Cruise and Tom Hanks. They can be relied upon to guarantee the successful opening of a Hollywood film. However, the association of any A-list star with a film project improves its chances of being financed and marketed successfully.

Stars are also increasingly keen to become involved in a film's production, not least because doing so gives them greater creative control over their career. Tom Cruise was able to select his personal choice of action director John Woo for *Mission: Impossible II* by co-producing it. Although somewhat less famous, Queen Latifah acted as executive producer on the comedy *Bringing Down the House*, a huge hit with US audiences if not with the critics. 'There weren't too many out there with a street credibility, and me and my team took out all of the jokes that were too racist. Not just the black jokes but Asian and Latino,' she claimed. But not everyone thinks that stars' pet projects are a good idea: the consensus on Sandra Bullock's *Miss Congeniality* was that it would have been a funnier film if the star had not tried to act as her own producer.

The conventional belief in Hollywood is that stars sell movies. According to Peter Bart of *Variety* magazine, 'Stars today aren't really actors, they're franchises, they're brand names. They know if they say "yes" to a project, then a $100 million project may roll into action.' Stars are the only element that can guarantee a film gets a green light. They can open a movie that would not have opened so well otherwise. Denzel Washington commented: 'More and more now I'll get a script before the filmmaker will get it or I'll be involved with hiring the filmmaker.' Every year the studios chase a handful of stars to fund their big movies — the blockbusters that are expected to return so much money that they will pay for all the flops and keep the studios solvent for another year.

Key words

first look contract; exclusive contract; housekeeping deal; script treatment; the pitch; high-concept film; investors

Film production

Most studios have overheads of about $300 million a year, so they have to make more than $300 million profit every year, otherwise they lose money. The return on investment in Hollywood in 2001 was about 4–5%. They would have made more money if they had simply put the capital into the bank and not made any movies!

Costs

The average cost of making a Hollywood blockbuster, including its marketing, is now roughly $100 million, so studios are not inclined to take risks. Even a medium-sized studio picture without big stars currently averages at a cost of $40–50 million: *The Fast and the Furious* cost 'only' $38 million to produce.

Any project made by untried talent or without a big name actor on whom to focus an advertising campaign will face an uphill struggle to be 'green-lighted'. For a short time in the early 1980s, video sales were the salvation of low-budget films. However, from the end of that decade onwards a recognisable star has also been needed to make it to the A-list shelf of high-street stores. Subsequently, the same has been true of DVDs.

Titanic went so far over budget that at one point the studio boss shut it down. *Titanic* cost Fox $150 million: right up to its release, no-one knew whether it would float or sink, but it was to become the biggest grossing movie of all time ($1.8 billion worldwide).

If something goes wrong during production, the chances of box-office success can easily evaporate. Production takes up to 15 hours a day, 5 days a week, for 12 weeks on average. Money is spent at a rate of up to half a million dollars a day: every minute not taken up with shooting costs money.

Screenwriters have noticed a change in the business in the last few years. Stars, particularly those being paid $20 million a picture, now have an enormous amount of creative control over the film.

Independent productions

It is possible to make films for relatively small amounts of money. The success of films such as *The Blair Witch Project* have made this not only workable but, more importantly, hip and acceptable. Two films by British director Mike Figgis — *Timecode* and *Miss Julie* — were each made for less than $4 million. Figgis is eager to promote the idea that, because of advances in digital technology, it is now easier to make a film on a small budget. He set up his own company, Red Mullet, determined to keep it as small as possible, and claims that it has the technical ability to compete with the big studios. It has enough equipment to make and edit films, together with a recording studio in which many of his recent films' soundtracks have been recorded and mixed. Figgis argues:

> In my opinion, it's not possible to be happy and courageous and work for a studio. But you can get very rich as a studio executive. This is not so good for filmmakers, however. Directors can earn plenty of money without needing to be rich and powerful. The minute you take the big studios' money, you have tacitly agreed to take their process seriously — which includes having to listen to some 33-year-old junior executive giving you his ideas about plot development and 'character arc'.

Studio executives rarely have the courage to go out on a limb for a film. Those who do seldom survive. *Fight Club** is an example of a high-risk movie that cost a chief studio executive — Bill Mechanic of Fox — his job.

Independent producers are always in danger of being swallowed up by the major studios, partly because of the stranglehold the majors have on distribution: they not only have access to the best venues and dates for release but are also able to keep their cinemas filled with their own products. Even if the film is not very good, at least it belongs to them (see later sections on distribution and exhibition for more explanation).

Jane Campion /Nicole Kidman, Piers Brosnan

Tip When completing your notes for this revision section, try to find your own examples of stars and directors who have their own production companies. How much control does owning the production company give the star/director over the film being produced?

Currently fashionable genres

> Serious filmmaking in Hollywood has reached a crossroads; will studios continue to put money behind 'grown-up' films or will it rely on high-return animations, mega-franchises such as Harry Potter and James Bond, and disposable teen detritus?
>
> (Bonnie Greer, *The Mail on Sunday*, 22 December 2002)

Whether you agree with this critic or not — and she represents a substantial body of opinion — you have probably also noticed during your film-going experience that at any given period, certain types of film are more likely to be playing at the multiplex than others.

Superheroes

Hollywood set 2003 as cinema's year of the superhero. As well as saving the world from evil, these comic-book characters were battling to become champion of the box office. Given that budgets for these blockbusters were running as high as $100 million, a great deal was at stake.

But was their success ever in doubt? Perhaps unsurprisingly, two of the most bankable releases — *The Matrix Reloaded* and *X2* — were sequels. There was also a strong charge from *Hulk*. The first cannily timed and explosive trailer for the film was screened during the Superbowl in January. It dramatically enlivened expectations for the film as the Hulk was glimpsed throwing a tank across the desert (would he finish the second Gulf War by himself?). Oscar-winning director Ang Lee (*Crouching Tiger, Hidden Dragon*) said of his part-hero, part-villain protagonist: 'I want Jackie Chan in Arnold Schwarzenegger's body.' Not satisfied with the idea of employing a 'real' bodybuilding muscleman to be the Hulk (as in the 1970s television version where Lou Ferrigno played the brute — he has a cameo role in the film as a security guard), advance publicity concentrated on how Lee relied almost entirely on computer-generated imagery, with the results being proclaimed to have raised this rapidly developing art form to new levels of sophistication.

Daredevil had been something of an obsession for director and screenwriter Mark Steven Johnson, who chased down the rights for more than 6 years. Risky casting decisions (Jennifer Garner as the love interest Elektra and Colin Farrell as the villain's sidekick Bullseye, neither of whom were household names at the time of casting) threw doubt on its chances, and reviews were often scathing. However, *Daredevil* quickly proved to be a worldwide hit. The film took almost £30 million on its opening weekend in the USA and the UK.

The X-Men first appeared in *Marvel* comics in 1963. Over four decades, with often as many as a dozen X-Men-related comics released each month, a complex web of interlinking stories has been created, only a fraction of which is touched upon in the films. It is the biggest selling comic in the world, bigger than either *Superman* or *Batman*. If its fans liked the movie, word of mouth alone would make it a hit. If they didn't, Fox would pay the price. A storm of fan criticism rained down from the internet when the cast list was announced: you can please some of the people some of the time, but you can't please all of the people on the internet! However, *X-Men* by and large satisfied the fans, and after the original's spectacular opening weekend in the USA (£33 million) and ultimate worldwide gross of £185 million, Fox got its money back many times over and *X-Men* became one of the hits of the year. *X2* was guaranteed. The original cast and director Bryan Singer duly signed on.

Martial arts

Bulletproof Monk (released in April 2003 in the UK) is another example of cult-comic mythology turned into a movie. The fight scenes made spirited use of the kind of Hong

Kong Chinese stunt work popularised by *The Matrix* — heroes running up walls, twirling in the air and freeze-framed in gravity-defying poses.

Monsters

Universal Studios came up with a neat solution to the problem of where to find a lucrative property — raid its back catalogue. It owned the rights to a 'stable' of monsters which had featured in its classic horror movies of the 1930 and 1940s:

- Boris Karloff's *Frankenstein* and *The Mummy*
- Bela Lugosi's *Dracula*
- Lon Chaney Jr's *The Wolf Man*

Universal first revived their monsters in 1999 with *The Mummy*, a blockbuster which made more than £250 million worldwide and led to two sequels. *Van Helsing*, a £100 million epic, features Count Dracula, Wolf Man, Dr Frankenstein's monster, Dr Jekyll and Mr Hyde, and the arch enemy of Dracula, Dr Van Helsing, played by Hugh Jackman, star of *Swordfish* and *X-Men*. Universal pencilled this in for release in May 2004 in the '*Star Wars* slot' — the time now traditionally reserved for films that are expected to be major box-office hits. (Another big production scheduled for release in May 2004 is DreamWorks' *Shrek 2*.) No doubt Universal are hoping that *Van Helsing* will be the start of a new series of films. George Lucas's special effects company Industrial Light and Magic, which of course worked on the *Star Wars* films, was on board to create computer-generated visuals.

Hybrid genres

Increasingly common are examples of **hybrid genres** which mix, for example, action and science fiction or action and thriller genres in order to gain the biggest potential box-office profit.

Tip You should do your own research into genres that dominate the cinemas at any given time. Try listing the films available at your local (multiplex) cinema. Which genres are on offer to the film viewer? Are there any genres that seem to dominate the list? If so, why do you think this is?

Key words

production company; hybrid genres

Film distribution and exhibition

Distribution

Distribution involves acquiring a film and trying to make it reach the widest possible audience, by selling it to **exhibitors** (i.e. cinemas). Just to break even at the box office, a film must make about two and a half times its initial development and production costs. The **distributor** usually aims to make 20–25% of the film's profits.

A distributor can acquire the distribution rights to a film in three ways:
- by investing in it
- by buying the rights after it has been made (in particular, independent films with smaller budgets may need to attract a distributor post-production)
- by being on board all along as a division of a bigger company responsible for both production and distribution (such as a major Hollywood studio which might be part of a multinational company)

The distributor's job includes planning how many prints of the film to make and negotiating the timing of a film's release with exhibitors. Each celluloid print costs approximately £1,000 to make and transport to an individual cinema. The major distributors in the USA and UK are UIP, Buena Vista, 20th Century Fox, Warner and Columbia Tristar. Worldwide distribution is predominantly US-based, dominated by Paramount, Warner, Walt Disney, 20th Century Fox, Columbia (though now owned by the Japanese company Sony) and Universal. These companies are simply new versions of the old Hollywood studios, now characteristically part of international conglomerates with interests across the entertainment industries and beyond.

Test screenings

Every major film is test screened before release. Almost since the dawn of the studio system, producers have believed that they never really have any idea whether the whole film works until it is put in front of an audience. Usually, someone outside a cinema hands out about 500 tickets to a private screening of a film due to be released in about 3 months' time. The audience does not know what movie they are going to see, they just know it will be a new film from a major studio. The test audience is asked to respond to a number of key questions about the movie, including:
- Did they understand the film?
- Did they like the star?
- Most importantly, would they recommend the film to a friend?

Test screening can prove beneficial because the audience may spot something that filmmakers too close to their product did not. Narrative inconsistencies and superfluous scenes can then be cut. Tim Bevan, producer of *Notting Hill* and *Bridget Jones's Diary*, sent female staff to sit with the test audience and even go into the ladies' toilets to overhear the instant reaction! Both ploys provided information. Such data are used to fine-tune movies before release through a combination of re-shooting and re-editing.

The studios are so protective of their investment that they are very secretive about test screening. Leaks in the press or on the internet can cost them dearly. The studio executive in charge of the test screening of Fox's *Independence Day* was so worried about the possibility of internet spies that he even kept the location of the test screening secret from Dean Devlin, producer of the film. In the event, the preview test audience in Los Angeles was so ecstatic that the studio knew that they had captured 'lightning in a bottle'. *Independence Day* went on to take $800 million at the box office, making it the most successful film of 1996.

Test screenings give the audience real power over Hollywood: the feedback can mean whole new scenes being created. Ronald Bass, scriptwriter of *My Best Friend's Wedding*, starring Julia Roberts, likes the testing process. He claims that audiences are cleverer and more sensitive than filmmakers. When the test audience saw *My Best Friend's Wedding*, they did not like the Julia Roberts character scheming to stop her best friend from marrying Cameron Diaz. This, given that Roberts was the top female box-office draw, caused the Sony studio great anxiety. Ronald Bass met with the producer and director to come up with some extra scenes to solve the problem, even though this involved the studio in some expensive re-shoots. One additional scene, in which she apologises to Diaz's character, gives Roberts's character a moment of redemption as she 'tries to make the world right again'. With six new scenes in place, *My Best Friend's Wedding* went on to become one of the biggest hits of the year, taking $287 million at the world box office.

Marketing

Studios spend almost as much on advertising a summer blockbuster as they do on making it. Sums from $50 million to $100 million on worldwide promotion are now commonplace.

Promotional images of any movie tell the audience what to expect. Marketing campaigns that do not work are more obvious than ones that do work. *The Mexican* starred Julia Roberts and Brad Pitt together for the first time and the posters showed them in a romantic clinch. But the studio was promoting a product they did not have. It was not a romantic comedy — Roberts and Pitt did not spend much time together on screen and the time they did spend was taken up with bickering and fighting. Word of mouth spread quickly and audiences stayed away in droves.

The attraction of A-list stars usually makes marketing easier. Their presence alone is often enough to attract people into the cinemas. However, it can also create problems.

> *The Mexican* was always meant to be an interesting, quirky, small movie, but how do you market a movie that has Julia Roberts, Brad Pitt and James Gandolfini from *The Sopranos* in it and 'platform' it out in a couple of theatres? They couldn't do that.
>
> (Lawrence Bender, producer of *The Mexican* and *Pulp Fiction**)

In this case, the filmmakers and the marketeers pulled in different directions. It was the attraction of the stars that gave *The Mexican* the green light, but it was their star power that caused box-office problems. The marketing messages had become confused.

Producers become frustrated when they know they have made a certain type of film, but the studio wants to sell it in a different way because it is not sure that it will bring in the audience.

The studio's attitude will always be: 'It doesn't matter what we do to bring them into the theatre, if they like the movie, they like the movie.' But as a filmmaker, if you feel you've made really good Chinese food, then you don't want to be selling the audience a pizza, because if they come in the mood for a pizza then no matter how good the Chinese food is they're not going to like it.

(Dean Devlin, producer of *Independence Day* and *Godzilla*)

Publicity

Posters and press junkets

Most campaigns start with a poster. For the public, it is the first glimpse they are likely to see of the movie. Posters raise awareness, but it is the press and publicity that bring an audience in.

Tip Try to include some of your own poster analysis in your notes. You may be able to refer to these examples in the exam. When analysing your chosen poster(s) you should comment on the following:

- genre elements — including props, actors, settings
- use of stars — who is in the film and how are they being used to market the film?
- the target audience
- use of intertextuality — does the poster include any references to other films, books, television programmes or music tracks? If it does, then how are these elements being used to sell the film?
- the **unique selling point** (USP) — what is special about this film that will make it particularly attractive to potential audiences?
- composition — how is the poster organised? Are certain images dominant and, if so, why?

Studios spend millions wooing the media at **press junkets**. Stars and directors are parked in hotel rooms for the world's media to be wheeled in to obtain soundbites. The film's publicists control the allotted 5-minute interviews with military precision, in order to ensure the maximum publicity in the shortest possible time. It is in stars' contracts that studios have to publicise the movie. Occasionally, a studio has spent so much on a movie that it tries to curry favour with extraordinarily lavish media junkets. Disney studios were hoping that *Pearl Harbour* would be the next *Titanic*, so they sent first-class air tickets to 200 journalists with invitations to fly out to Hawaii for a publicity party aboard an aircraft carrier. There they were wined and dined, sung to by Celine Dion and were allowed to mingle with and interview the stars of the film. Disney spent $5 million on this publicity stunt, but it seemed to encourage mainly negative **reviews**.

However, the studios cannot control all publicity. Harry Knowles runs a website called **www.aint-it-cool-news.com**, on which movie journalists and on-set production staff can post stories that would otherwise lose them their jobs, and audience members can e-mail their test screening experiences of future releases. Knowles then publishes these, free from the influence of the Hollywood spin-doctors. The studios would like to prevent this 'revenge of the audience', as one executive put it. The website, with its huge — mostly young — fan base, has become a major irritant to Hollywood. Warner Brothers accused Knowles's spies of sabotaging *Batman and Robin*, starring George Clooney; MGM's remake of *Rollerball* was previewed by Knowles with particular savagery. However, the studios have recently adopted the tactic of exploiting the site's hip, cult reputation to their own advantage. Posters for *The Hunted*, which opened in the UK in June 2003, carried a single quotation, courtesy of **www.aint-it-cool-news.com**: 'A non-stop, unflinching assault'.

Studios are having to spend more and more money just to persuade people to watch their films. Advertising costs have gone up 800% in the last 20 years. Clever marketing teams are always looking for a new angle, which increasingly involves merchandising.

Merchandising

Merchandising really took off with *Star Wars* in 1977. It sometimes brings in more than ticket sales. *Spy Kids*, the children's adventure, benefited from an unusual piece of enterprise by director Robert Rodriguez. Most family films — indeed most blockbusters — are remakes of old projects (*Batman*, *Spider-Man*, *X-Men*). However, *Spy Kids* was not a known property and studios are reluctant to green light a project where there is no pre-existing public awareness. Rodriguez made a rough trailer and, 2 years before the movie was due to be released, took it to McDonald's. The international fast-food chain signed on because it could see that the film would appeal to its audience — kids/families — and that the tie-in would be commercially beneficial. This huge promotional support made it seem a bigger picture, because the 21 million people entering a McDonald's every day saw the movie being advertised 'for free'. In a 3-week period, up to 650 million people were exposed to the movie, which went on to take $144 million at the US box office.

Tip Try to add some merchandising examples you have noticed to your notes.

Festivals and premieres

Generating a buzz of publicity for a movie is a gamble. One difficult decision for Hollywood studios is whether to risk sending their latest pet projects to a major film festival before release. The Cannes Film Festival remains the most prestigious in the world. Hollywood studios are deeply suspicious of it, perceiving the French critics to be hostile to big-budget, commercial films, particularly those from Hollywood. Why run the risk of failing, especially when the glare of the international spotlight is upon you? DreamWorks studio head, Jeffrey Katzenberg, was anxious about premiering their irreverent animated movie *Shrek* at the Cannes Film Festival in 2001. However, there was an extraordinarily positive reception to the film from the Cannes audience and the gamble ended with an Oscar in 2002, for best animated movie.

Screenings at festivals gain international attention and media coverage. The director, actors and producers attend to meet critics and journalists and to generate a 'buzz' around the film. The leading festivals are held annually in Cannes, Venice, London, Berlin, Edinburgh and Park City, Utah (Sundance). There is an increasing number of smaller but significant festivals, such as Cambridge. The Berlin festival is in February and tends to be a sober, dignified launch pad for Oscar-potential Hollywood films and European art films. With an air of sophistication and none of the hype of Cannes, stars have started to gravitate there in growing numbers. Venice in September has some European art films and plenty of Hollywood premieres, with all the major studios giving large talent-attended parties.

Classification

Before a film can be screened to a paying audience in Britain, the distributor has to arrange and pay for it to go to the British Board of Film Classification (BBFC) for certification. Distributors know that the level of certification is vital when targeting an audience, because it determines the age at which the marketing has to be pitched. Audiences for mainstream films tend to be young, so the lower categories are generally thought to be more commercially beneficial as they maximise the potential audience. Distributors do not want an unexpectedly high rating at this late stage and they may well seek advice from the BBFC. For example, the distributors of *Spider-Man* wanted a '12' certificate for the film in the UK, and some of the more graphic scenes were cut to achieve this.

The timing of release

Today, in the age of internet gossip and well-publicised advance rumours, the actual release of the film is the culmination, rather than the beginning, of the whole marketing process. In the USA, the first weekend can now account for as much as 60–70% of a movie's takings.

According to studio bosses such as Warner Brothers distribution chief Dan Fellman, 'People have got to see the movie the first weekend they can. After that, the frenzy is over.' However, some critics argue that the studios realise that any movie that bottoms out so spectacularly in its second weekend is one that has been 'found out' by intelligent moviegoers. A week is about how long it takes for the hype-wave to crest and disperse, for the bad word of mouth to spread and for the takings to plummet accordingly. Such sceptics cite as evidence the box-office charts for summer 2001. Every weekend there was one clear leader among the new releases, which in turn was toppled by another blockbuster movie that lacked the staying power to last more than a week at number one. For example, *The Mummy Returns* sold $68.1 million worth of tickets in its first three days, followed by less than half that in its second week. Similarly, *Jurassic Park III* dropped off by 56% and *Planet of the Apes* by 60%. *Pearl Harbour*, *Swordfish* and *Lara Croft: Tomb Raider* all opened hugely and then fell away.

There are, of course, exceptions to the rules. Sometimes audiences can make a film much more successful than the distributor has predicted, as happened with Baz Luhrmann's *William Shakespeare's Romeo + Juliet* in 1997. There are still more examples of what are known as 'sleeper' hits — films that start relatively small and get bigger and bigger through word of mouth.

Front loading

There is a recent studio marketing tactic in the USA known as 'front loading' — it is *expected* that a movie will make most of its revenue in week one. Studio distributors claim that it is possible to 'buy' an opening weekend if they are willing to pay for it. Saturating all television stations with fast-moving commercial trailers for the last 10 days before a movie opens persuades people to go out on Friday and Saturday to see it.

Every studio aims for a huge opening weekend. Being top of the charts for just 1 week is enough to kick-start a global campaign. Even if this is followed by a rapid decline in receipts, the film is up and running. A good opening weekend in the USA for a big movie is anything from $30 million upwards, although *Spider-Man*'s $115 million raised the bar. Even with a massive drop-off in audiences, the film is likely to reach the magical $100 million mark within a couple of weeks.

Compressing such a huge percentage of the potential box office into one weekend has an added commercial advantage for the studios, because of what independent exhibitors — cinema operators — regard as an unfair arrangement between themselves and the studios in the early weeks of a new release. Studios normally give 50% of the box-office receipts to the exhibitors, but on the opening weekend the studios pocket up to 80% of the takings. Everything rides on the opening weekend — the entire studio management can be sacked for one failed blockbuster!

Key words

test screening; marketing; publicity; unique selling point; press junket; merchandising; festivals; premieres; classification; timing of release

Exhibition

Exhibition is the point in the film's journey when it is released into cinemas. The film is shown in either an art house or a mainstream (multiplex) context. However, the type of cinema in which the film appears is not the only thing you should consider when discussing exhibition.

Reviews

If exhibition means exposing the film to the audience, then this includes reviews and criticism. Distributors try to provide press kits for journalists, including photographs and cast interviews. They arrange film festivals and other types of premiere, such as royal galas, in order to generate publicity. However, distributors cannot ultimately control or finally determine the review process. The domino effect caused by a wave of negative criticism is unstoppable.

However, while critics handed out some scathing reviews for the summer blockbusters of 2001, more importantly for Hollywood, during the summer of 1999, the US public spent a record amount, breaking the $2.7 billion high set in 2001. The critics universally sneered at Disney's *Pearl Harbour*, but the studio was delighted by the final takings of $451 million. *Planet of the Apes* (Fox) received another critical drubbing, but took $358 million worldwide. Almost all reviewers over the age of 16 hated *Lara Croft: Tomb Raider* — nevertheless, it managed to make a respectable $275 million. *Artificial Intelligence: AI* produced and distributed by Warner Brothers, and directed by Steven Spielberg, performed badly at the US box office but picked up well in the rest of the world, finally taking $236 million. DreamWorks' animated feature *Shrek* was the top summer film of 2001, earning $476 million. It was the only hit movie of that summer to be applauded by the critics. Most of the studios were ultimately satisfied with their returns, although, with the exception of *Shrek*, they had received damning reviews and had fallen short of audience expectations.

There have been widely reported fake reviews invented and paid for by the studios, which were also captured on video marshalling junior members of their marketing teams into acting as satisfied moviegoers in staged television promotional commercials. This manufacturing of bogus critical opinions by the major studios led some independent distributors to tout themselves, with what they in effect advertised as complete, unexcerpted reviews on their posters, plus websites where an interested audience could read further unexpurgated, uncensored reviews. That was the tactic first adopted by the distributors of *Sexy Beast**, a British film that was one of the imported-to-the-USA surprise hits of the summer of 2001, and which continued to do good business for the rest of the year. So good reviews do mean something after all.

Tip Look at a number of reviews of the same film, from different publications. What do you notice about the way the film is discussed and the elements of the film that are focused on? Can you tell the potential audience from the content of the review?

Multiplex chains are keen to take the credit for the resurgence in film audiences, arguing that although blockbusters such as *Harry Potter* and *The Lord of the Rings* have helped bring in the paying customers, it is the transformation of the whole cinema experience that has really attracted them. Advertisers are certainly attracted by multiplexes because of the make-up of the audience — mainly young, upmarket and with a high level of disposable income.

Video and DVD rental

When VHS videos became widely available in the UK in the early 1980s, it was confidently predicted that pre-recorded tapes would kill cinema. In fact, while cinema admissions bottomed at 54 million in 1984, they have climbed steadily since, reaching 156 million in 2001.

Meanwhile, the number of videos hired for home viewing fell from the 1989 peak of 289 million to 162 million in 2001. The value of the market fell by 36% in real terms over the same period. The picture looks a little brighter for the rental business when figures for DVDs are included. By the end of 2002, just 4 years after their launch, about

14% of British homes had a DVD player. This number is increasing significantly, as high street prices fall and accessibility widens, and PCs, Macs and games consoles are made with built-in DVD players. In 2001, 25 million DVDs were hired, boosting the total value of the rental market to £464 million.

Key words

reviews; art-house cinemas; multiplex cinemas

Case study

Donnie Darko has been chosen as a distribution and exhibition case study because it is an example of a successful attempt by a small, enterprising, independent UK distributor to market a US 'indie, art-house' film to British audiences.

Donnie Darko was marketed in the UK by Metrodome, an art-house, independent distributor that normally plays to niche audiences. In recent years, Metrodome has successfully distributed some non-mainstream, and even controversial, films in the UK. Examples include *Chopper**, *Together* and *Human Traffic**. However, of the 12 or so films they release a year, only one is likely to be a hit, for reasons largely to do with the success of films produced and distributed in the UK by major US studios.

US distribution and exhibition

Donnie Darko was first screened at the Sundance Film Festival as an 'indie, art-house' film. However, because it seemed to contain science-fiction type special effects and featured Patrick Swayze (although no longer the huge box office attraction he was in the days of *Dirty Dancing* and *Ghost*), the film disappointed 'indie' audiences who were expecting a more alternative experience, produced outside the Hollywood format.

The US distributor who then picked it up targeted a mainstream, teenage horror, multiplex audience, setting a cinema exhibition release for Halloween 2001. This also flopped because these US audiences were expecting a slasher, 'teenie kill' movie along the lines of the *Scream** franchise.

You will remember the importance of a successful opening weekend if a film is to continue being exhibited on the competitive US screens. The 'word of mouth' on *Donnie Darko* was generally negative. In addition, the timing of the film's release was most unfortunate, occurring only a month after the terrorist attacks of '9/11'. A film including a plane disaster was unlikely to soothe the raw sensibilities of US audiences.

Meanwhile the film was being shown at a series of the leading film festivals, including Berlin, Cannes, London, Toronto and Los Angeles. These international festivals also function as auctions to encourage a variety of distributors, who can bid for the rights to a particular national market. Metrodome had seen *Donnie Darko* at the Los Angeles film festival in February 2002, by which time the asking price for the UK distribution rights for release to cinemas, airlines, video/DVD and eventually television had fallen from £1 million to £100,000 because of its failure at the US box office. Metrodome decided that the film had been mishandled by the US distributor's marketing campaign and bought the rights.

UK distribution

Setting *Donnie Darko* for an October 2002 release, Metrodome needed to decide on its marketing budget in relation to the target audience. Therefore, the film was screened to various industry audiences to help gauge its likely appeal — not only to Metrodome's own marketing department and the outside agency it hires to design its posters, but also to selected press and radio journalists. Press support would be vital to secure publicity in the form of column inches, because a small distributor such as Metrodome cannot afford the huge advertising campaigns used by studios and larger distributors. Radio is an increasingly important medium in Britain due to expanding audiences, with critics such as Mark Kermode on Radio 5 Live and James King on Radio 1 wielding significant influence. Luckily for Metrodome, Radio 1 called *Donnie Darko* 'the best film of the year'. Together with other favourable comments from broadsheet newspapers and listings magazines, this encouraged Metrodome to increase its marketing budget and arrange for repeat screenings to film magazines such as *Total Film*, *Hotdog* and *Uncut*. Rave reviews would follow: 'Genius...film of the year' (*Total Film*) and 'Restores faith in the US indie scene' (*Uncut*).

Advertising

Metrodome eventually spent £80,000 on advertising *Donnie Darko*, much less than the £2,200,000 spent by another distributor at the same time on the so-called indie hit *My Big Fat Greek Wedding*. Metrodome positioned the film as a 'twisted, clever, genre-defying, late-night, cult, up-market, review-led movie'. (Bad reviews in news-papers may not make much difference to the success of blockbusters, because the marketing of these films is so well planned.) *Donnie Darko*'s target audience was more likely to respond to reviews, especially in broadsheets, than to cinema trailers or advertising on television, which Metrodome could not afford. However, a national advertising press campaign was still essential. Metrodome believed it had a film by an exciting new young director, with a strong script, supported by some excellent US reviews and growing UK publicity. If handled skilfully, *Donnie Darko* had the poten-tial to be a 'crossover' hit, the dream of every independent producer or distributor who has a non-blockbuster film and does not want to see it play to a restricted art-house audience.

London Underground campaign

A significant portion of the advertising budget (£15,000) was spent on the London Underground campaign which ran for a month until the end of the summer. The poster for this included press endorsements and quotes from film magazines, together with a venue strip at the bottom giving the addresses and telephone numbers of the cinemas playing the film in London. There was also a quotation from the BBFC guidelines warning that *Donnie Darko* 'contains strong language and psychological horror', which Metrodome seized upon gratefully because it was more likely to attract than repel their target audience. Furthermore, it suggested clearly what kind of film to expect — that is, not mainstream.

Main poster campaign

The main poster campaign changed the image from 'scary cinema' to 'odd, surreal cinema' and displayed clearly for the first time members of the cast sitting in an auditorium alongside the 'rabbit' figure from the film. There was also a quotation from a positive review by Jonathan Ross to reassure potential viewers that *Donnie Darko* was not too art-house.

Guerilla marketing

An intriguing development in advertising a would-be 'cult' film like *Donnie Darko* is a 'guerilla' marketing campaign — although distributors would never admit to this, because it is illegal. Guerilla marketing involves street-level advertising using graffiti, stickers, fly posting and leaflets. For example, a mural on view during the Notting Hill Carnival, or a huge, blank billboard on Clapham Junction filled for a month with an 'unofficial' design for the film, might cost only £100.

Publicity

Given its limited marketing budget, Metrodome knew that cast support would be vital for publicity. A PR company was hired to help position the cast and director for the press. However, the 'big', already established Hollywood guest-stars were unavailable. Drew Barrymore was a co-producer of the film as well as featuring as the rebellious teacher, so Metrodome was hoping that she might conduct publicity interviews in person for the UK release. However, she was engaged in the production of the sequel to *Charlie's Angels*. In the event, she managed some telephone interviews. Patrick Swayze was simply 'too busy'.

Fortunately, Jake Gyllenhaal, the young lead actor, happened to be in London appearing in a play and so was 'hot' in terms of publicity. Moreover, Metrodome would not have to pay him to fly over from the USA and stay in a hotel. He did some press and photo shoots in April for magazines such as *The Face*, *ID*, *Sleaze Nation* and *Attitude*, which are all publications whose influence far outstrips their low circulation because they are read by 'style leaders'.

Targeting a wider audience, the front cover of *The Sunday Times Culture Magazine* was also secured. This was an important coup.

The director, Richard Kelly, was brought over from the USA at a cost of £10,000, including flight, accommodation and expenses/pocket money. He did mini-junkets for press interviews and question and answer sessions at screenings of the film, leading up to the UK opening. The 1980s-themed premiere cost another £10,000. However, with no glamorous stars available to appear on the night and attract press coverage, it was not as useful for publicity as the kind of star-studded gala event held for Hollywood blockbusters.

Merchandising and promotions

These were limited to the Radio 1 campaign. Metrodome paid Radio 1 to hire the cinemas where the film was screened to their listeners.

UK exhibition

The marketing and promotional campaign was reinforced by a carefully orchestrated theatrical release pattern.

Opening

Donnie Darko opened on 30 screens in the UK on Halloween 2002, a full year after its US debut. On multiplex release was *Halloween: Resurrection* and *K-19: The Widowmaker* — not strong competition, given that Metrodome's target audience would be likely to regard the former as a tired extension of a franchise long past its sell-by date, and the latter as a feature for an ageing star (Harrison Ford).

A standard blockbuster release would be 400–500 screens, whereas a typical art-house release would be only four or five screens. Half of the prints were shown in London art-house cinemas, which traditionally take up 50–75% of this kind of 'platform' exhibition. Many films still open in London before the rest of the country, which helps exhibitors get their bookings right. However, for *Donnie Darko* only one exclusive print was released in other major cities, such as Manchester and Liverpool. This was because showing a film on a single art-house screen can create more positive word of mouth and give it a chance to build an audience. Because of whom they attract, art-house cinemas are seen by independent distributors as a better forum for 'buzz' resulting from people discussing a new film and influencing others to see it.

Screen average

The screen average is the average number of tickets sold per screen. Distributors check the returns for the opening weekend on the Monday — a strong performance will reassure them that the film will still have a screen on the following weekend. In fact, distributors usually know from the first Friday whether the film will succeed or not.

The screen averages for *Donnie Darko* were excellent because of the positive word of mouth. After 2 weeks, an extra 25–30 prints were struck to hit multiplex screens. *Donnie Darko*'s screen average was second only to *XXX*, the major Hollywood release starring Vin Diesel. There was even pressure on Metrodome to increase quickly the positioning of the film to 150 or so screens. However, this was resisted because Metrodome believed that it was more important to have relatively fewer screens sold out than to have more screens half empty. Only that way would audiences return to the cinema to see it the following week and word of mouth would be built upon successfully.

Video and DVD sales

Donnie Darko took a total of £1.6 million at the UK box office, over three times the amount initially projected by Metrodome when the UK distribution rights were bought. Such a substantial figure was important in giving the film a high profile in readiness for the video/DVD release on May 19 2003. This had another strong advertising campaign, including full-page advertisements in film magazines, such as *Total Film*, *Hotdog* and *Uncut*. These stressed the special features available on the DVD. Among other extras, the 20 deleted and extended scenes, with optional director's commentary, were targeted at those already committed fans who had seen the film at least once in the cinema. There was also a promotional tie-in with the HMV chain, offering a limited edition sleeve plus six 'art cards'. Metrodome might be able to keep about 35% of the profits from the film, the rest going to the producers, but might retain as much as 85% of the revenue from video/DVD sales.

Television rights

Metrodome sold the television rights to the BBC for £250,000 — although initially, when the film had a lower profile, the BBC did not want it. Metrodome will keep about 50% of the revenue from this and from the airline rights. For a small distributor such as Metrodome, selling the television rights is essential to cover marketing costs.

However, the expanding television markets have both advantages and disadvantages. The newer digital channels such as BBC 4 are particularly important when it comes to buying foreign language films. Sky has its own output deals with the US studios, and terrestrial Channel 5 has decided to buy in recent major studio blockbusters, alongside its customary presentation of afternoon television-movie re-runs and late night soft porn — Metrodome's distribution is unlikely to find exhibition there.

Total profit

The total profit received by Metrodome from *Donnie Darko* (just under $2 million) helped to offset the other 11 films they distributed in 2002 that, in relative terms, flopped at the box office.

The British film industry, then and now

Introduction

Hollywood has always been ruthlessly efficient at producing, distributing and exhibiting films. In 2003, cinemas in Britain recorded their biggest January audiences for 32 years, with a total of 16.3 million movie visits — 8% more than in January 2002. *The Lord of the Rings: The Two Towers* and *8 Mile*, starring rap artist Eminem, helped to make this the best start to the year since 1971. The Cinema Advertising Association predicted that a higher than usual number of blockbusters — including the sequels to *Charlie's Angels* and *The Matrix* — should push Britain's total audience for 2003 to around 182 million.

So, given that British audiences and exhibitors have a well-developed appetite for Hollywood blockbusters and for US films in general, how can the British film industry compete? In one sense, this is not a new story. The First World War virtually eradicated British production. Since then, the British film industry has been pronounced dead many times, only for it to be revived once more. The USA began to move in with most of the films that British cinemas required, maintaining an economic stranglehold through 'blind' and 'block' booking, which demanded exhibitors contract films sight-unseen and in bulk. The grip of these restrictive business practices was further tightened when US producers, who had already recouped their investment at home, were able to undersell British filmmakers. The introduction of sound intensified the competition from Hollywood.

Significant periods and genres

There have been significant periods and genres contributed by Britain to the history of world cinema, including:

- the 1930s documentary movement
- the 1930s British classics of Alfred Hitchcock
- the 'social realist' period (1959–63) featuring the talents of Lindsay Anderson, Karel Reisz, Tony Richardson and John Schlesinger

During the Second World War, British film production transformed itself from a sickly industry more or less ignored by both audiences and critics into one that achieved both box-office success and critical favour.

The mini-studio system

For nearly 50 years, the main source of commercial film production in Britain was the 'mini-studio' system, which was a scaled-down version of Hollywood. The most important of these studios included:

- Ealing (1938–59) — especially comedies
- Gainsborough — costume dramas of the 1940s
- Alexander Korda's London Films

However, all three of these 'quality-conscious' studios failed to build on early successes, probably by failing to adjust to changes in taste and economic climate. The *Carry On* series (1959–74) and Hammer Studio's horror films (1955–73) were commercially successful British **franchises** (a series of films based around the same actors or characteristics) which met a similar fate, for largely the same reasons. By the end of the 1970s, this form of 'mini-studio' film production had all but collapsed. British films were left to be funded on a more individual, one-off basis, with packages put together around the commercial potential of a particular property — a subject, a director or a star.

The British film industry has traditionally been in an awkward position — unable to follow completely the Hollywood studio model and unprotected by the state. It has been expected to survive commercially without any significant aid and subject to heavy competition from Hollywood.

What is a British film?

Should a British film have:
- been made in Britain mostly, or even exclusively, by British personnel — writer, director, production crew and actors?
- British subject matter?
- been made for a British audience?
- British funding?

The definitions of what makes a film British are varied and flexible. Legally, it should be:
- mostly made in Britain with predominantly British personnel
- mostly British financed
- 'projecting Britain' — a representation of aspects of the British way of life to address squarely the cultural concerns of British people, which today means taking advantage of the full social and cultural diversity of the UK

Investment in the UK

Where do producers go to obtain funding for British films? How do they secure it? These days, even so-called 'low-budget' British movies cost around £1 million to make and most will not even recoup their costs. Unless the producer is independently wealthy, it is a case of scrambling for money from a mixture of public grants, broadcasters, special film finance funds run by groups of investors and, just maybe, from rich investors cashing in on tax breaks.

The government

Historically, government funding for filmmaking in the UK has been small, but there have been more recent attempts to finance the industry through several sources, including British Screen Finance Ltd. This was a film investment company backed by both the state and private sectors. Its contribution rarely exceeded £500,000 and was never more than 30% of a film's budget. Nevertheless, from its establishment in 1986 to 2000 (when it was absorbed by the Film Council — see page 38), British Screen was one of the most important sources of finance for British films. It invested in over 130 films including *The Crying Game**, *Orlando*, *Naked*, *Land and Freedom* and *Butterfly Kiss**. For *Land and Freedom*, British Screen invested at an early stage of development, putting up money for research into the historical context, location finding and the next draft of script development. This allowed the producers to seek out other sources of finance in Europe. Eventually, there were 15 different sources of money for the film.

Lottery funding

The **Arts Council** channelled lottery money into British films in an organised attempt to nurture the industry. Film production in the UK had traditionally been a series of small cottage industries, with individual, independent producers working on their own. The idea was to integrate and consolidate the producers into a new mini-studio system by:

- encouraging a raft of British film production rather than a string of British films
- allowing the creation of three groups of people — collectives of directors, producers and other film personnel — who, through their 'virtual studios' and their franchises, would have the near certainty that they would have a substantial amount of public money available to them for 6 years

The lottery money would always be a minor investment in the films themselves but it would contribute to building the infrastructure of a proper filmmaking business, rather than there merely being the artistic ambition to make one film after the next, with producers having to start afresh to find money for their next project. Lottery funding would be used to attract other finance in order to complete a budget for a film.

Criticism of lottery funding

Critics of lottery funding argued that 'throwing money' at scripts and producing films would simply mean adding more films to the shelf of unseen British movies. More films would be produced simply because they *could* be and less attention would be given to the development of strong screenplays. Too many films would fail because they had nowhere to go.

The Arts Council was criticised for investing in the loss-making end of the industry (production) when it could have bought some of the chains of cinemas that were available at the time, such as the Cannon chain, bought by Richard Branson of Virgin. Then it would have had a constant flow of money that could have been used to promote production of British films that might have had a greater chance of exhibition.

The funding structure

Others were critical of the funding structure itself, believing it was helping from the wrong end, because it is first-time, independent producers who have the hardest time breaking through. These are the people who would like to keep the British business going and who are prepared to risk money on a good script.

Some observers go so far as to say that it is difficult to become a producer without a private income, and that even if you are in the established producers' loop it is possible to continue to make films without any of them being any good. They argue that one of the reasons why there were so many lottery-funded 'turkeys' was because of the clique of producers and financiers who were in charge of handing out the grant money.

Most lottery money was granted through the film panel of the Arts Council, a now disbanded collection of appointed producers and film-finance experts who inevitably had connections with several of the production deals that they funded. For example:

- Colin Leventhal of Hal productions was a member of the Arts Council panel. His film *Mansfield Park*, a joint BBC Films venture with the US giant Miramax, was one of those to benefit. It received a £1 million grant and, while some critics welcomed the film, it is hard to see why a commercial project with such big backers should have been given public funds.
- Premila Hoon was also an Arts Council panellist at the time that she was orchestrating the film investments of Guinness Mahon. This company put money into two fairly successful projects, *Wilde* and *Shooting Fish*, which also received big lottery grants.

Both Leventhal and Hoon declared their financial interests at the time.

Success rate

Between 1996 (when lottery money became available) and March 2000, about 130 feature films received lottery backing. Of these, only nine could be described as successful. Many had fallen at the last hurdle and were still awaiting distribution deals, while others were permanently on hold.

Relative box-office successes that received grants included the acclaimed Mike Leigh film *Topsy-Turvy*, *Hilary and Jackie*, *Hideous Kinky* and *The Land Girls*. There were true critical successes too, such as Lynne Ramsay's *Ratcatcher*, which would not have been made without lottery funding.

The Film Council

The **Film Council** was set up by the government in April 2000 and is now the main source of funding for many British films. It absorbed the existing sources of government assistance, including the Arts Council's Lottery Film Department and British Screen Finance. The Film Council manages and allocates public funds and grants set aside by the Department of Culture, Media and Sport for the film industry. This includes lottery money, the amount of which varies with ticket sales. Some lottery money is still administered by the three co-partnerships created previously by the government — the Film Consortium, French-owned Pathé Pictures and London-based DNA. The Film Council's funds aim to provide start-up finance towards the development or production of films. They are not intended to back a film fully.

The Film Council's three main funds (collectively worth £20 million annually) are:

- The Development Fund — £5 million per year to help get screenplays into better shape before production. This was set up in response to the frequent criticism that too many British films were being rushed into production before their scripts were properly developed.
- The New Cinema Fund — £5 million per year aimed at 'cutting-edge' filmmaking. This money is primarily for feature films and projects that exploit new technology, with a particular focus on work from regions outside London.

- The Premier Fund — £10 million per year, concentrating on putting money into the wider process, including identifying those films with the potential for international distribution and marketing.

Local and regional funds

A large part of the Film Council's remit is to encourage regional and ethnically diverse projects. There is a range of local organisations with funds to dispense. The Council invests £6 million a year through the Regional Investment Fund for England. Many regional groups, including Scottish Screen, The Northern Ireland Film Commission and The Arts Council of Wales, have joined forces with regional broadcasters to generate additional finance.

Television companies

Television companies have been seen as the most important source of funding for British films since the 1980s, although television investment in the UK has been low compared with that of major foreign television companies, such as HBO (USA) and Canal+ (France), over the same period. The attraction for television companies is that in addition to the hoped-for financial return on their investment, they receive the broadcast rights after the film has been released in cinemas. The rapid increase in the number of television channels and the arrival of pay channels (satellite, cable and digital) has led to more demand for films.

Channel 4

Since its launch as the fourth UK television channel in 1982, Channel 4 has supported more than 300 films, including many key British films such as *My Beautiful Laundrette*, *Riff-Raff*, *The Crying Game**, *Four Weddings and a Funeral*, *Shallow Grave**, *Brassed Off* and *Trainspotting**. Borrowing from the examples of German and Italian television, Channel 4 has supported the production of feature films by offering full funding, equity investment or the pre-purchase of television rights. The Film Council's funds have become even more important following the closure of Film Four. This was Channel 4's film studio, which was merged back into the television station in July 2002.

BBC Films and the ITV companies

Channel 4 gained cultural prestige from its filmmaking policy. This was particularly important when it was struggling to establish its identity against the three existing television channels and it also encouraged the competition to become involved, to varying degrees, with film production.

Generally, the ITV companies did not fund film production. However, some noticed Channel 4's critical success and began to make investments. For example, Granada Television co-financed *My Left Foot*, which was Oscar-nominated for Best Picture. However, Granada Films folded in Autumn 2002.

BBC Films has a relatively small budget of £10 million per year to make lower-cost feature films. It hopes to make more films for around £500,000. However, its mission is to find new talent. It runs schemes working with new producer/directors and writers and it has a large development team to whom scripts and treatments can be sent.

Funding and the future

The recent cash cuts by broadcasters have had an impact on funding possibilities, especially for less well-established producers. There are also fresh obstacles, for both new and established producers, in obtaining finance from big US studios. The studios, now largely part of huge multi-media conglomerates burdened by debt caused by the economic collapse of the dot.com boom, are less ready to take risks. As sources for novice filmmakers have dried up, projects built around joint financing from the Film Council (co-funded by the Treasury and the Lottery), regional funds and television companies may be the best way for newcomers in Britain to get started.

Problems and weaknesses of the British film industry

We have seen that there is a long-standing problem of persuading distributors and exhibitors that British films are worth showing and that they will find an audience, especially as they have to go out of their way to promote a British film, particularly if it is an independent one. By contrast, US films tend to enter the British market with print and advertising money behind them.

Arguably, a truly British film industry needs an infrastructure whereby British films could be developed, produced and distributed nationally and internationally, without European and US finance. There is a strong argument for putting more money into distribution in the UK, because distributors — particularly independent ones — are in competition with wealthy multinational companies which own most of the distribution outlets (i.e. the cinema screens).

Other problems

There are other reasons why Britain has found it difficult to have a 'real' film industry:

- In general, US stars seem to have been more acceptable (more glamorous?) to British audiences than British ones. (Can you think of any exceptions? Do you think this is still true?)
- The British theatrical establishment has had a snobbish attitude towards film actors. Even when there has been crossover between the two industries and stage actors have done film work, the assumption has been that they did it just for the money and not for artistic respect. (Do you think this is still true? Consider recent performances such as that of Sir Ian McKellen in *The Lord of the Rings*. Conversely, why do British film actresses such as Kate Winslet — or Hollywood stars such as Nicole Kidman and Gwyneth Paltrow — continue to try to become accepted as respected performers in London stage productions?)

- Generally, the arts establishment in Britain has seemed to look down on film. When arts subsidies eventually started, film was regarded as somehow less worthy of support than, for example, opera or live theatre.
- Attracted by better creative facilities and higher pay, there has been an export of talent to Hollywood. This includes successful directors, such as Alfred Hitchcock, Ridley Scott and Sam Mendes, and actors such as Sean Connery, Ewan McGregor, Kate Winslet and Catherine Zeta Jones.

Language

Another point — so obvious that its significance might be forgotten — is that we speak the same language, more or less, as Hollywood cinema. British cinemas and television channels (and more recently video/DVD outlets) have been well supplied with English-speaking US films. The British are notoriously reluctant to learn other languages and have never been *obliged* to watch dubbed or subtitled films. A producer once claimed that: 'if the United States spoke Spanish, Britain would have a film industry'. Do we really need a film industry in Britain, however much we think we might like one?

'Britishness'

There has been a suspicion that much recent mainstream British cinema has pandered to clichéd US expectations of what constitutes 'Britishness', in a cynical (or desperate) attempt to make films more suitable for export. In the 1980s and 1990s, British audiences at the multiplexes became used to seeing often distinguished British actors being cast as villains in Hollywood blockbusters (think of Jeremy Irons in *Die Hard: With a Vengeance* or Alan Rickman in *Robin Hood: Prince of Thieves*).

More recently, in British movies there has been a shift in the representation of class and character, although again created with aspirations to achieve success in the global marketplace. There have been two tendencies:

- First, there was the comic vision of middle-class English incompetence on display, originating with the success of *Four Weddings and a Funeral* and developed in *Notting Hill* and *Bridget Jones's Diary*. All three films involve the star Hugh Grant and Britain's most successful scriptwriter, Richard Curtis, and all were successful at the US box office. Indeed, the latter two romantic comedies were US/UK co-productions. It seems that Hollywood and US audiences prefer to view the British as endearingly useless, bumbling but 'sweet'.
- Second, there is a tendency to represent British working class culture and masculinity as essentially violent, criminal but 'cool'. The revival of the classic British gangster movie *Get Carter** and the US success of Guy Ritchie's *Lock, Stock and Two Smoking Barrels** — the latter a highly stylised mixture of comedy-violence and gangster-farce — inspired a host of poor imitations, such as *Circus**, *Fast Food** and the BBC-backed *Love, Honour and Obey**.

However, there is an argument that the great temptation in the film business is the idea that bigger is always better. Part of the problem is the phrase 'the British film industry', with its connotations of mass employment and large studios (such as

Shepperton–Pinewood, now partly owned by the British film director brothers Ridley and Tony Scott) booked for years ahead. Producers get nervous when sterling is strong, because the Americans might take their dollars elsewhere.

Key words

franchise; lottery funding; the Arts Council; the Film Council

Film consumption: the cinema audience

Film consumption is an area that should not be thought of as separate from film production in this exam. Films are produced for an audience; they are products that are sold to consumers. The film industry uses many strategies to encourage you to spend your **leisure pound** (the money you reserve for entertainment) at the cinema. Your discussion of film consumption will form a part of the answers you give in both sections of the exam. To be certain that your revision notes are complete, make sure that you cover the following questions: 'who?' 'how?' 'why?' and 'where?' For the 'who?' section of your notes you will need comments that define different audience groups and their viewing habits. For your notes that cover 'how?' you should look at the various technologies by which an audience might consume film. To address the question 'why?' you should identify what motivates an audience member to choose a particular film and the expectations and preferences that that individual brings to his or her viewing. The question 'where?' invites discussion of the contexts in which consumers view films, whether in the cinema or at home.

The audience

Audience profiles

For any discussion of audience profiles or audience groups, you should remember that you are a film viewer and therefore have essential experience as a consumer. Your own viewing history, present preferences and expectations should form an important part of your answers. Are you an active film **fan**, someone who is a member of a film-related fan club? Do you post reviews on internet sites, in order to share your opinion of a film? Do you have particular film preferences that dictate what you choose to see?

You could interview older members of your family. Ask them about their experiences of cinema-going, as this information could provide a useful reference point in your answers. You could conduct your own investigations into areas of debate, such as

whether or not mainstream film audience members and independent film viewers are entirely different from each other. You will not need to do any detailed demographic investigation. However, you should identify key pieces of information in your notes, such as the fact that most cinema-goers are between 14 and 25 years old. As this is the age group that provides most box-office revenue, you will need to debate whether this affects the type of films produced for the mainstream market.

How audiences view films

For investigations into how audiences view films, you could begin by using the viewing technologies (DVD, big screen technologies and the internet) listed in the 'Film and new technologies' section of this guide (see pp. 48–54), and consider how these have changed both the way we view films and our expectations of the formats on which we can view them.

Pose yourself questions and answer them in your notes. Do the options available on a DVD encourage the consumer to break their watching of the film itself with 'excursions' into the extras provided? Is the **immersion experience** of watching a film at an IMAX cinema different from or better than the standard film viewing experience? Is the internet now the main source of film-related information for the consumer? You will need to consider whether the expectations of technology are as important as the actual content of the film for the viewer.

Why audiences view films

It is an interesting question as to why audience members view particular films. Individuals have preferences and expectations, but you need to go beyond this and consider how those preferences and expectations came about.

A film consumer may be drawn to particular genres. If so, this could be because of long-term exposure to the genre, which is then viewed out of habit. It could be because a genre is fashionable and therefore gives a certain status or social standing to the viewer.

Films may become intriguing to the potential consumer because of successful advertising campaigns or because they have earned cult status, perhaps because of a ban or a controversial issue. A particular star or director attached to a film might make it attractive to an individual.

In order to consider why a film is attractive to a consumer, you will also have to discuss the idea of 'constructed' audiences. Films may imply appropriate audiences through their content or marketing campaigns. Consider, for example, the term 'chick flick'. If this is attached to a film by producers or critics, it implies a female **target audience**, which wishes to go and see a film that either mirrors some part of the female experience or includes elements (such as romance narratives), which women supposedly prefer (e.g. *Calendar Girls*). Make sure that you identify and make notes on any film marketing campaigns that you think are defining the audience.

Where audiences view films

The issue of where an audience member sees a film connects with discussions concerning cinemas and home consumption. From your own experience, and that of your peer group, you will have a good idea of how many times the young adult viewer goes to the cinema.

You might answer a question that asks you to reflect on the role of the multiplex cinema and you could analyse why these multi-screen complexes are so popular. Is it because they offer convenience, choice and a whole evening's entertainment? You could look at the films offered at an independent cinema and those shown at your local multiplex and discuss the differences and similarities in audience profile.

Consider the fact that, in the mid-1980s, the number of people who went out to the cinema was at its lowest ever, but today numbers have increased dramatically. Is this because of:

- a greater range of films offered now?
- an increase in film quality?
- an improvement in the cinema environment?

Or is it because film technology has advanced to the point where even the most sophisticated home entertainment systems cannot match it?

Where a film is seen also raises the question of with whom. If a film is viewed on DVD or VHS, at home with friends, then there may be a difference in the way an individual responds to the film than if he or she were alone. The types of film viewed at home by groups of peers might differ from those they choose to see at the cinema. There are age limitations on films. This legislation is more difficult to enforce within the rental market than it is at the cinema. Films transferred to video or DVD are often more heavily cut or given a higher certificate to try to stop underage viewing. Viewing a film in a cinema is a collective experience and some consumers prefer to be part of an audience rather than a sole viewer.

Conclusion

Consider the 'who', 'how', 'why' and 'where' questions when you are making notes on film consumption. They will help you to focus on particular areas, which can then be applied to questions in the exam. Remember that producers and audiences are interlinked and affect each other. Both are active within the film industry and within the topic of film consumption. Film companies may try to construct a potential market for their film through advertising campaigns. Audience members can also affect the industry by reviewing films on the internet, spreading opinion via good or bad word of mouth or opting not to see types of film they consider no longer fashionable.

Key words

leisure pound; fan; immersion experience; target audience

The star system

The term **star system** concerns the role of stars within the film industry. Your discussion of the star system should concentrate on three areas:

- How the role of the star has changed since the days of the Hollywood studio system.
- How the industry uses stars within marketing strategies.
- The relationship between the star and the viewer.

Before tackling these three areas, you must first make sure that you can define a star and how a star is different from the rest of the acting community. There are a number of questions that you could use in your attempts to define a star:

- Is the individual **globally recognisable**?
- Does he or she receive wide media coverage? This coverage could be in the form of interviews, press releases, television appearances or newspaper articles about their personal life, as well as their career.
- Can this individual **open** a film? In other words, is the attachment of his/her name to a project enough to secure both pre-production investment and box-office success?
- Does he or she receive critical acclaim? Has he or she been awarded, or nominated for, industry awards, such as Oscars or Baftas?
- Does the actor or actress receive huge fees for film work? If so, it is because the film company believes in his or her ability to make a film a box-office success?
- Is the individual regularly associated with particular roles, which highlight a certain quality? For example, Arnold Schwarzenegger and Sylvester Stallone have become synonymous with action films, which trade on their physical presence.
- Does he or she have characteristics to which the viewer aspires? From the Hollywood studio days, for instance, you could identify actresses such as Greta Garbo and Marlene Dietrich, whose aloofness and beauty made them attractive to audiences.
- Is the individual someone with whom the audience can identify? A good example would be Tom Hanks, who often plays an 'everyman' character.

Use the questions above to help you not only identify a star, but to discuss which factors contribute to star status.

The changing role of the star

Stars in the golden age of Hollywood

During the golden age of the Hollywood studio system (1930–48), stars were 'owned' by particular studios for the 7 years of a particular contract. They made films only for that studio and starred in films the studio chose for them.

During this period, the image of the star was manufactured by the studio. Stars emerged out of studio 'stables' in which they were 'groomed' and taught to walk, speak and live in a manner defined by the studio. Stars were chosen from those actors and actresses who existed within these 'stables'. Their images were carefully fashioned by the studio, in order to project a certain type of presence to the audience. Clark Gable, Gary Cooper, Humphrey Bogart and Jayne Mansfield were all stars whose images were created in this way. Clark Gable was presented to the cinema audience as a romantic leading man and was given roles such as Rhett Butler in *Gone with the Wind*, which secured this image. Gary Cooper was predominantly associated with the role of the honourable lawman, the man of integrity who would reinstate order and peace to a troubled town; *High Noon* provided perhaps the ultimate vehicle for this image.

Although stars within this system were guaranteed to make a certain number of films a year, they were not always satisfied with their role as studio product. They did not have artistic freedom and many were unhappy with being placed in a series of similar roles, which would ultimately **typecast** them.

Stars today

Stars today also have the problem of being typecast, but they are not under the same contractual pressure as their predecessors. They may find their niche within a particular genre or role and be expected by the industry and the audience to deliver what they are best associated with. However, there is a choice of films available to them.

Contemporary stars have much more control, not only of the films they choose, but often over the content and direction of these films. Their presence is so potentially lucrative for the producer that stars can often influence the production choices within a film. Today, the amount of money an actor or actress's films gross at the box office is a deciding factor in their star status. Tom Cruise, for example, has never won an academy award, but his box-office success secures his star status.

The industry's use of stars

The star can provide an essential part of a producer's marketing strategy for a film. In terms of promotion, the producers of a film will let press representatives have biographical information about the star, which they hope will invite interest from the public. For example, a story about a star's rise from obscurity can make potential viewers interested, because of the implication that anyone (even the potential viewers) has the ability to succeed if they have enough drive.

Good, and even bad, publicity around a star can have the effect of keeping him or her in the mind of the audience. Considering contemporary society's thirst for celebrity information, even stories about bad behaviour can be beneficial to the producer, if they encourage interest and box-office takings.

The press machine behind a star is enormous. With the impending release of a film, the star will be called on to undertake a promotional tour. This will include press interviews, appearances on everything from talk shows to film review programmes and high-profile attendances at premieres. The star may be asked to record interviews for DVD releases, or to take part in a 'behind the scenes'/'the making of...' short film.

For the industry, stars are at their height when their films make profit. During a period of maximum public interest, stars often appear in more than one release a year. For the industry, the presence of a star in a film is essentially a marketing bonus. Individual stars have fan clubs and the kind of dedicated fan base that producers hope will translate into box-office revenue.

The relationship between the star and the viewer

The viewer's perception of a star

The star exists for the viewer in films and also in the press coverage attached to the star. Therefore, it is worth bearing in mind that the viewer will have mixed ideas about what a star is really like.

The viewer's perception of a star will be mostly fixed by the roles the star takes on in a film. If the star repeatedly plays the same kind of role, or often appears within the same genre of film, then the viewer will attach certain expectations to that star. If continuity of response is broken, by a star appearing in a role or type of film that the viewer does not associate with him or her, then the viewer's expectations may not be satisfied. Arnold Schwarzenegger's detour into comedy roles in *Twins* and *Junior* was greeted with disapproval by some fans, who were used to his muscle-bound physique appearing in action movies. Meg Ryan has become synonymous with romantic comedies and audiences expect the combination of vulnerability and quirkiness that she brings to roles within this genre. Would the pleasures of watching a Meg Ryan film be lessened if the predictable genre and character traits were absent?

Identifying with stars
The ability to **identify** with stars and the roles they play is often an important part of the viewer's response. If the viewer is able to empathise with the plight of a star's character and identify with the issues being dealt with, then the star becomes more accessible and therefore more attractive.

Idolising stars

Idolising stars from afar, **aspiring** to be them or to have their lifestyle, might also be part of the viewer's response. The aloofness, unattainability and mystery of stars, which existed in the Hollywood Studio era, is almost impossible in today's society. We have all kinds of information about stars through extensive press coverage.

Star persona

Another interesting idea that you could incorporate into your debates is that of the **star persona** as a 'blank canvas' onto which the viewers project their hopes, dreams and fantasies. This suggests that the star provides an opportunity for the viewers to live outside their usual existence. A viewer might watch *Ocean's Eleven* and dream of a relationship with George Clooney or Brad Pitt, or be an avid Bond film fan because of a secret fantasy to live the life of the special agent. In these cases, the character's look, attributes and actions have encouraged viewers to bring their fantasies to the viewing experience.

Key words

globally recognisable; to open a film; typecast; identification; aspiration

Film and new technologies

New technologies have had a significant impact on film production and consumption in recent years. The filmmaker can now choose to produce a film on celluloid or digital video (DV) tape. The consumer's experience of films now includes those made with computer-generated imagery (CGI), those produced on DVD and those produced with big screen (notably IMAX) technologies. Unit 2 questions tend to concentrate on key areas connected with new technologies. Questions concerning the film industry might ask about the impact of certain new technologies on the production, distribution or exhibition of films. Questions that concern audiences might focus on the different consumption practices that new technologies invite or the change in viewing expectations caused by the advent of new technological advances. This section highlights key new technologies and their impact on both the producers and the consumers of film.

The internet

The internet is a global computer network, which provides access to roughly a billion pages of information on the web. Millions of homes have access to the internet and to any information relating to film that is available on it. For the film industry, the internet has become central to the marketing of its products.

Official websites

Any mainstream film that you see advertised at the cinema will have its own website. Many smaller, more independent films will also have their own sites. Before a film is released, the website will include information on the cast, the filmmakers and the film itself. The site may provide a synopsis of the plot, trailers and clips from the film. For the fan or potential viewer, the site provides pre-release information from which they can decide whether or not to see a film. Discussion boards on a website can make the potential viewer feel part of the film's **viewing community**.

Marketing advantages

For the film distributor in charge of marketing a film, there are numerous advantages to a website. In comparison to a poster campaign, cinema trailers or press advertising, a website is relatively cheap; websites that sell merchandise can be almost self-financing. A website can be continually updated, so any new or amended information is easily added to the site's content. The number of 'hits' on a website and the number of downloads taken from it give the distributor an idea of the potential interest in a film and may help predict box-office takings. In terms of targeting audiences, the main consumers of film are aged between 14 and 25 years, as are the main internet users. The distributor can therefore 'speak' directly to the target audience.

Unofficial websites

While official websites provide an important marketing tool for the distributor of a film, unofficial sites have a slightly different function. These sites are apparently unconnected with the filmmakers and provide a forum for fan reviews, gossip and unauthorised information.

Positive **word of mouth** is extremely important for a film's box-office success, and unofficial sites are a useful indication to the distributor of the pre-release response to particular films. Adverse, or negative, fan reviews posted on unofficial sites can be damaging to the word of mouth surrounding a particular film and are extremely disconcerting for a distributor.

Insider information

Certain fan sites might include 'insider information' collected from individuals on the film set of a particular film or from trade magazines not available to the public. This kind of information can have a significant impact on the potential consumers' response to an upcoming release and may sway their opinion. However, it is worth remembering that unofficial websites are not immune to the influence of the film industry. Cynics might suggest that it is the industry itself that 'plants' certain intriguing or controversial stories on fan sites, in order to increase interest in a film.

Marketing lower-budget films

The internet can provide a relatively inexpensive forum for marketing lower-budget films. Independent filmmakers, who have produced a film using digital cameras and editing programmes, can create their own websites and upload promotional images, clips and details. Therefore, the huge population of internet users can be targeted without the enormous marketing budgets of the major distribution companies. *The Blair Witch Project* is a perfect example of a lower budget film that used the internet very successfully before the film's release. The internet teaser campaign for the film, which posted information about a seemingly real event, inspired the kind of positive word of mouth that is invaluable for a film's marketing campaign and eventual box-office success.

Digital versatile discs

Although digital versatile discs (DVDs) have been available for some years, they remain interesting to discuss in relation to both the film industry and the film consumer. DVDs have seven times the capacity of a standard compact disc and can therefore hold far more than just a film text. They often include scene analyses, storyboards, behind-the-scenes information and director's commentaries, as well as the film itself.

DVDs and the film industry

For the film industry, there are many advantages to this technology. When films were first available on DVD, the quality of the images and sound was often poor. However, today's DVDs contain a quality of image and sound that often exceeds that of VHS films.

For the industry, DVDs have now become a second format on which to market film. The revenue once gained purely through VHS recordings can now be added to by lucrative DVD sales. It is not just new releases on DVD that prove profitable for film companies; back catalogues of classic films re-released on DVD provide huge sales. Seduced by promises of increased quality and extra features, consumers who already own copies of a film on VHS might also buy the DVD copy. There is also scope for releasing special extended editions, such as those of *The Lord of the Rings*, as well as the original theatrical cut. The space on a DVD allows the addition of more trailers for films produced by the same company and thus provides scope for the marketing of other film products.

The only potential problem for film producers is the recordable DVD and the impact that this might have on sales.

Synergy
Here, **synergy** is defined as the promotion of two connected products from the same company. It is enhanced by the DVD format. If the film production branch of a parent company has produced a film and the music branch of that same company has released a tie-in track, then both can be housed on a DVD. This allows both products to be promoted through the same format.

DVDs and the consumer

For the consumer, DVDs offer not only a different package of viewing material, but also a potentially different viewing experience. The addition of institutional information (e.g. behind-the-scenes reports, cast interviews and director's comments) and pre-production information (e.g. storyboards), gives a wider package of information than merely the film. Viewers can gain knowledge of the production elements of a film, as well as 'readings' of a text by the cast and director. However, directorial commentaries raise an important issue and you should be aware of the potential of these commentaries to offer a preferred reading (one from the filmmaker), which might influence an individual's response to a film.

Computer generated imagery

Computer generated images (CGI) are those that have been created on a computer and then added to a film. Some films use CGI to recreate elements that would otherwise be too expensive to produce. For example, in *Gladiator*, the cityscapes of Rome were created by CGI technology, as were many shots of the ship and its passengers in *Titanic*. Other films can be remastered by adding CGI elements. Jabba the Hut, a character from the original *Star Wars* trilogy, was created in CGI for the re-release of the films and then added to the original footage. For some films, the unreal or fantasy elements may now be created using CGI. The dinosaurs of *Jurassic Park* and the character of Gollum from *The Lord of the Rings* are CGI creations. The audience has no living example with which to compare these creations, so the limitations of CGI in the production of reality are not an issue. Examples of films created solely with CGI include *Shrek*, *Toy Story* and *Monsters, Inc*.

CGI and the film industry

CGI has many benefits for the film industry:
- The cost of building enormous sets can be avoided by creating a setting using CGI.
- Films can be reworked with CGI elements to maximise potential buyer interest in a film they may already have purchased.
- Films driven by special effects can be made even more exciting and dynamic.

Companies such as Industrial Light and Magic, established by George Lucas, now have an extremely successful position within the film industry. However, it must be remembered that the advent of CGI has not completely taken over from traditional animation. Nick Park's *Wallace and Gromit* films have had both popular and critical success and are made using entirely stop-motion animation techniques.

CGI and the consumer

In terms of the film consumer, CGI provides an interesting area for discussion. Your comments on this new technology should consider:
- the impact of CGI on the expectations of the viewing audience
- whether the inclusion of CGI elements provides a sales tool for the industry
- whether audience members choose to see a film because of the CGI elements

If a film does not have CGI components where a contemporary audience might expect them, does this lessen viewing pleasure and adversely affect audience expectations?

Big screen technologies

There have been many types of big screen film viewing experience over the last century. In the 1950s, Cinerama was popular with audiences and provided a technology in which films were shown on large screens, often in widescreen. 20th Century Fox then introduced CinemaScope to the viewing public, which was marketed as a much more exciting and realistic film experience.

IMAX

Today, perhaps the best-known form of big screen experience is IMAX. This is an integrated system of film production that uses cameras, film stock, screens and projection equipment especially designed to offer an exciting, live experience. With a projector the size of a small car, screens the size of three double-decker buses and film stock double the size of the film industry standard of 35 mm, IMAX film production is very different from its traditional relative.

IMAX and the consumer

The experience of IMAX is quite unlike the standard film-going experience. Usually the films available in the IMAX format are non-narrative. They offer an experience (of being under the sea, in space, on the moon etc.) or are a showpiece for the technology (three-dimensional films and animated spectacles, for example).

There is a debate as to whether the audience could contend with a 2–3-hour narrative piece. The IMAX film experience is one of immersion. It offers huge, digital, surround-sound systems and images that enter the front and peripheral (side) vision, creating a total physical viewing experience. Would an audience be able physically to withstand this for longer than the usual hour of an IMAX film?

There are attempts to transfer successful mainstream films onto an IMAX format. *The Lion King* is one example of a film primed for IMAX release.

IMAX and the film industry

For the industry, the possibility of IMAX exhibition outlets could mean increased revenue.

Video and computer games

Playing video and computer games is an extremely popular pastime. Most games are played on either a PC or a games console, such as Playstation 2, Gamecube or X-box.

Video and computer games and the film industry

The popularity of the computer games industry can be exploited in various ways. If there is a pre-existing consumer base for a certain game, then a film of that game will have a potential audience. The makers of the *Tomb Raider* films and *Resident Evil* would certainly have hoped to trade on the established popularity of the games. Such games not only have pre-existing characters, but scenarios, settings and even basic narratives that can be used as the basis for a film.

It is not just as a resource that video and computer games can be beneficial to the film industry. As an avenue for merchandising, they can be very lucrative. The spin-off games from films such as the *Harry Potter* series and *The Lord of the Rings* trilogy provide a huge potential for ancillary (extra) profits.

Video and computer games and the consumer

For the film consumer, the recent release of films that began life as computer games raises different issues. A game-user might be considered by the industry to be a fairly safe potential film viewer. However, the attraction of a game may not merely be the images or the stories it contains. The interactivity of the game experience is not yet something that can be replicated within the cinema experience. If being able to interact is the unique selling point of a game, then the viewer might be disappointed by the film.

Tip This point might not be a significant factor in prohibiting the success of films derived from games, but it would provide you with an interesting topic for debate in the exam.

Digital cameras and editing software

The shift from analogue to digital technologies has been one of the most significant developments over the last few years.

Digital cameras, editing software and the film industry

For the film industry, the effects of this shift have been numerous. For established filmmakers, there are new options for filming equipment. Digital cameras are usually more portable than their traditional counterparts, editing suites are often smaller and the copying of films is cheaper and easier with DV tape, which does not produce ever-worsening copy quality.

Advantages

The kind of digital equipment used within the industry differs from that which individuals might buy for themselves, but many of the advantages are the same. Mainstream filmmakers (such as George Lucas, with his *Star Wars* instalment, *Attack of the Clones*) have adopted this technology in the production of films for a mass market.

Once a film has been transferred to a celluloid print it is costly and time-consuming to make any changes to it. A film produced on DV tape can be altered much more easily, as the digitised images can be extracted from the tape, uploaded onto a computer, altered and then loaded back onto the tape.

Problems

The issue for filmmakers, with regard to distributing a film on DV tape, is that not all cinemas have digital projectors. The exhibition outlets (cinemas) need to be able to show a digitally produced film for the digital filmmaking process to be complete.

Digital technology and lower-budget films

The advent of digital processes has encouraged the production of lower-budget films by filmmakers who do not have the same level of resources as the big companies. With cheaper cameras available and the possibility of editing on a computer, a film can be produced for a fraction of the cost of using traditional film equipment. For example, *The Blair Witch Project* is a low-budget film, made entirely with digital cameras, which eventually achieved mainstream success.

For the film consumer who is also a budding filmmaker, there is the possibility of creating a product without a huge budget. The internet could provide a means of distribution, and even exhibition, for a low-budget, digital film. Websites can be created relatively simply and can provide a medium in which to advertise a film; sections of the film can be uploaded to advertise the product further.

Key words

viewing community; word of mouth; synergy

Questions
&
Answers

This section of the guide contains questions typical of **Unit FS2: Producers and Audiences**. For each question, two answers are provided — one of A-grade standard and one of C-grade standard. It is important that you use these answers as a structure and content guide, rather than as model answers. You may choose to answer the questions quite differently, using other examples, and achieve equally good marks. Consider the language used in the answers and the way in which the material is organised and the arguments are structured. These elements will be of most use to you when you are preparing for the exam.

Examiner's comments

Each of the candidate answers is accompanied by an examiner's comment. These are preceded by the icon *e* and indicate where credit is due. In the weaker answers, they also point out areas for improvement. Pay particular attention to the skills highlighted in the examiner's comments and the problems identified. The examiner's comments should act as advice for you in your examination preparation.

The Hollywood film industry, then and now

Extract 1: Statistics showing how box-office figures in Britain have changed since the height of the Hollywood studio system

Year	Total audience (to nearest million)	Change in box-office numbers from 10 years before (%)
1950	1,396	—
1960	501	−64
1970	193	−61
1980	101	−48
1990	97	−4
2000	143	+47

Extract 2: A view of the characteristics of the new Hollywood 'blockbuster' film

The blockbuster, in contrast to the small-scale independent feature, is aimed at the popular audience in general, rather than at any particular section of the viewing population. It addresses this audience by means of a mix of genres — often combining action/adventure, with comedy, romance, science fiction and the like. Many critics argue that in comparison to old Hollywood, new Hollywood films are not structured on narratives based on cause and effect and on characters who are motivated and develop, but on loosely based action sequences built around spectacular stunts, stars and special effects.

(Adapted from Warren Buckland, *A Close Encounter with Raiders of the Lost Ark*)

How far do you think the up-turn in box-office figures in Britain in the last 10 years is the result of new Hollywood's focus on the blockbuster film?

Total: 25 marks

■ ■ ■

A-grade candidate's answer to Question 1

Britain's cinema audience has risen in the last 10 years. This could be due to the number of multiplex cinemas opening across the country each year. With more screens, and films showing for only a few weeks, audience figures are bound to rise. Cinemas are often within shopping 'malls' and next to fast-food outlets. So going to the cinema can be more than just a 2-hour experience; it might even be part of a whole day's entertainment. This is appealing to consumers and has affected the number of people going to the cinema in the UK. For years, the Hollywood film industry has been making films with a wide audience appeal. These are called blockbusters. In extract 2, it says: 'The blockbuster...is aimed at the popular audience in general, rather than at any particular section of the viewing population.' A film with mass appeal, such as *Titanic* or *Armageddon*, is bound to have a much greater chance of box-office success than a smaller production, such as *Donnie Darko*.

Extract 2 goes on to comment on blockbusters as 'often combining action/ adventure with comedy' and as revolving around 'loosely linked action sequences, often built around spectacular stunts, stars and special effects'. *Armageddon* fits this description exactly. The stars of the film, Ben Affleck and Bruce Willis, were used to sell the film. The dramatic special effects featured heavily in the trailers for the film and were another sales ploy. The trailers for the film began to appear during the Christmas period of 1997, although the film was not released until the following summer. The pre-release marketing of the film was elaborate and no doubt extremely expensive and the potential audience was promised huge-set action sequences and sophisticated special effects. The film appealed to all ages as it was organised around thrills and action. The storyline was simple and would therefore have global appeal — there were no lengthy monologues or sophisti-cated themes, which might be difficult to translate abroad.

Studios spend millions of dollars on the films themselves and the marketing budgets of blockbusters are also huge. Teaser trailers, main trailers, merchandise and posters introduce the idea of the film to the public long before the actual film hits the screen. The word of mouth generated by the marketing campaign of block-busters often creates a 'must see' buzz about the forthcoming film.

Overall, I do think that blockbusters have had an effect on British box-office figures in the last 10 years. However, I do not think that they are the sole reason. Blockbusters do make the cinema experience more accessible to a wide audience and the stars used in blockbusters are certainly a draw. Advertising is relentless and often makes it impossible to ignore a forthcoming blockbuster, and special effects contribute to larger audiences. However, the advent of new technologies, such as the internet, has also contributed to a rise in British cinema audiences. The amount of information available on the internet about films is massive. You can download trailers, discuss films in chat rooms and access interviews with the stars. Audiences now have more access to information about forthcoming films, and the film industry has a perfect context in which to advertise.

The experience of a whole day's entertainment in shopping malls, where consumers can shop, eat and then finish their day with a film, is also a major factor affecting growing British box-office receipts. Today, seeing a film is not such a rare occurrence. Many people will go to see whatever is showing at a multiplex so that they can enjoy a relaxing evening after a hard day's shopping.

🖉 This answer shows excellent understanding of both extracts and their part in the debate surrounding the rise in British cinema-going. The candidate has used relevant examples to substantiate points and has extended the arguments implied in extract 2. This answer is succinct and challenging. The candidate has extended the argument beyond the literal into a debate concerning other factors that might have affected British cinema audiences. This is a clear and accurate response, gaining 22 out of 25 marks.

■ ■ ■

C-grade candidate's answer to Question 1

Over the last 10 years, there has been a dramatic increase in visitors to the cinema. The total audience number in 2000 was 143 million compared with 97 million in 1990. This 47% increase would seem to suggest that Hollywood's focus on the blockbuster film has had a large impact on box-office figures.

The blockbuster is aimed at a much wider audience and combines many genres in one. This means that it does not target a specific audience, but a wide range of potential viewers. For example, *Titanic* contained something for everyone. Since new Hollywood began to focus on the blockbuster, more films have been released that follow a formulaic pattern. This makes the films fit with the audiences' expectations. They are not surprised by what they see and can have an easy, predictable viewing experience.

However, blockbusters may not be the only reason for a rise in British box-office figures. Between 1950 and 1960, cinema audience figures were extremely high, as people would often go to the cinema two or three times a week. This was more as a social event, rather than just to see the film itself. They also had a larger disposable income available as the war had finished, so they were able to fund going to the cinema. This may be what has happened since 1990 as the cinema has become more of a social occasion, with the introduction of multiplexes. The multiplex has snack bars and other facilities for people to use after or before they go to see a film. Another possible reason is the advance in both picture and sound quality. For example, with the introduction of surround sound, the whole cinema experience has become more realistic.

Overall, I would say that the blockbuster has had a large influence on the up-turn in cinema audiences, but it is not the only reason. There is a combination of reasons why Britain's inhabitants are going back to the cinema.

e This answer discusses the impact of the multiplex in some detail and proposes ideas for other factors that have been influential on the British box office. However, the candidate relies heavily on the extracts provided for other comments and gives only one, brief, example of a blockbuster. In order to comment effectively on extract 2, this example should have been expanded with comments identifying how *Titanic* 'fits' with the blockbuster definition offered in extract 2. Overall, this is an uneven answer in terms of argument offered and would score 14 marks out of 25.

The British film industry, then and now

There has been an on-going debate on the problems of the British film industry. In 1999, the Film Council suggested that the weaknesses of the industry included:

- an insufficient number of vertically integrated companies operating across development, production and distribution
- a failure to attract sufficient money from the financial markets
- a well-developed appetite among audiences and exhibitors for US films
- UK distributors who do not give priority to British films
- a lack of investment in script development, resulting in too many poor-quality films being made
- a continuing loss of British talent to Hollywood
- a failure to take advantage of the full cultural and social diversity of the UK

Using the material above and your own knowledge of the British film industry and its products, what do you consider to be the most significant factors holding back the development of financially successful and distinctive British films?

Total: 25 marks

■ ■ ■

A-grade candidate's answer to Question 2

The US film industry is the most profitable in the world. It has established world-wide audiences through its use of formula genre films and instantly recognisable stars. The British and US film industries share the same language and this provides the first hurdle to the success of British films. British films have much lower press and advertising budgets; therefore, they have a far smaller chance of global exposure. The budgets behind Hollywood blockbusters enable the use of sophisticated special effects and the employment of well-known stars. These two elements also contribute to a squeezing out of British films. British audiences are used to the high-concept US product, with high production values. British audiences can understand the language spoken in blockbusters. They have therefore been 'trained' to expect what is offered by the blockbuster and so, because of a combination of accessibility and habit, British audiences will often go to see a US product rather than a British one.

British films are not such a financial 'safe bet' as US films. Investors are seduced by film products that have already been proved successful. Blockbusters have their own conventions, such as huge action sequences, which invariably draw audiences in. Therefore, potential investors often finance US films because they have more chance of a good financial return. Getting funding for British films is a difficult process. Since the demise of Channel Four films and the government's reduction in film investment, the number of British films produced has declined.

Filmmakers in Britain often have to look to Europe for finance. For example, the makers of the 2001 film *Dog Soldiers* had to go to Luxembourg in order to complete the budget for the film. Not only are US blockbusters more of a safe financial bet, many US companies, such as Warner Brothers, have a vertically integrated system. Therefore, the films they produce have a pre-determined context for exhibition. UK companies are not vertically integrated. They do not have the means of distribution and exhibition under 'one roof' and have to look to other companies, which might not feel that a British film is likely to be financially lucrative enough either to distribute or to show in their cinemas.

The continuing movement of British stars to Hollywood is also a problem for the British film industry. In order to gain global success, stars have to 'make it' in Hollywood. Thus, there is a vicious circle. British films do not often gain global release, so the stars of these films only become famous within a limited context. Kate Winslet, Ewan McGregor and Catherine Zeta Jones are all British stars that started their careers within the British industry and have since gained global renown in Hollywood. However, some British stars do attempt to bring something back to the British system. Sadie Frost, Jude Law, Ewan McGregor and Sean Pertwee set up the Natural Nylon production company in order to try to produce British films, and Gary Oldman has, with *Nil by Mouth**, brought his name to a low-budget British production.

The irony has always been that Britain has the acting, directing and technical talent to produce extremely good films, but for some reason a British film industry is not something that has been encouraged by successive British governments.

This is an excellent answer, which draws on the source material and discusses key difficulties within the British film industry effectively. Thorough knowledge is shown of the impact of the Hollywood film industry on Britain and the candidate has incorporated his or her own relevant examples into the argument. This is a systematic approach to the question, which extends the source material in a challenging way, and is worth 23 marks out of 25.

■ ■ ■

C-grade candidate's answer to Question 2

The British film industry finds it difficult to develop and produce financially successful and distinctive films for a variety of reasons. One of the most important factors is the lack of intelligent funding. It takes money to make money in the film industry. There are exceptions to this rule (for example *The Blair Witch Project*), but generally speaking it is true. The British film industry lacks the money to produce blockbusters, which attract the widest audience to the cinema. Recently, the national lottery granted money to the film industry, but many feel that it was wasted on inexperienced directors and poor scripts.

Another reason why our industry is performing badly is the lack of Hollywood-style studios, which work across development, production and distribution. As there aren't any of these fully integrated companies, the cost of making films is higher and the profits a film makes are split across different companies. This means that companies are not making enough money to finance future projects.

The audience's taste for Hollywood blockbusters is also holding the British industry back. Blockbusters are designed to appeal to the widest possible audience, in order to make the most money. Most people in the UK, when going to the cinema, will be going to see a US film. This is a shame, because the only reason why these films are more successful is because they have access to large amounts of money. Hollywood spends a ridiculous amount of money on marketing its films.

The loss of British talent to Hollywood is also detrimental to the earnings of the British film industry. Many people say that one of the factors that make a successful movie is the star. Most British actors who want to make it big go to Hollywood, leaving behind many very good actors but not many famous names. People such as Catherine Zeta Jones and Jude Law are key examples of this.

To my mind, given a chance, the British film industry could be a force to rival Hollywood. However, without well-placed financial aid and integrated studios, Britain will always lack the means to market a film successfully. It is not the quality of films that is holding the British film industry back; it is the fact that Hollywood seems to have taken over British cinemas.

> The candidate has used the source material quite effectively and has chosen key points to argue. There are some perceptive statements concerning the factors that have impeded the British film industry and some useful arguments that extend what is implied in the source statements. However, the answer lacks concrete film examples to back up points and often arguments are left either unexplored or unsubstantiated. It would be awarded 15 out of 25 marks.

Film consumption: the cinema audience

The following are responses to the experience of viewing violent films, as recorded by Annette Hill in her 1997 study *Shocking Entertainment: Viewer Response to Violent Movies*.

- 'Quite often with violent movies, I put myself through seeing the film to see — can I brave this? Everyone else has gone to it. You are a wimp if you don't sit through it.'
- 'You go to the cinema or you watch it with others at home and you are very aware of other people's reactions. *Natural Born Killers**, it was banned. So you are watching it partly for yourself and partly to see how others react.'
- 'In *Braveheart*, a guy falls to his death and everyone laughed at that. I can't understand why I did that. I suppose you try and fit in with everyone else, so you don't feel left out.'

Using these comments as a starting point, discuss how the audience you view films with, and the circumstances in which you view them, may affect your response to the films that you see.

Total: 25 marks

■ ■ ■

A-grade candidate's answer to Question 3

This question asks us to consider the social contexts in which we watch a film, as well as the film text itself. The same people might give different responses in different contexts. This depends on distinguishing between the response of social groups, collectives of people (audiences) and the responses of the individual (the spectator).

Films are now viewed in many widely different contexts: at the cinema; at home on television (via an increasing number of channels on satellite and cable); on video and DVD; over the Internet; while travelling using a portable DVD player or laptop; on aeroplanes and so on. A viewer's response to the same film viewed in these different contexts may well be very different. The context of consumption and our enjoyment of a film changes depending on the social occasion and our mood — whether we are going to the cinema alone, on a date, for a night out with a larger group of friends, or with our family.

For example, consider a night screening outdoors, such as the free travelling roadshows set up in public parks or on beaches. Watching the cult film *Withnail and I* on Brighton beach with hundreds of fellow student fans (all of whom eagerly anticipate and quote most of the dialogue as it is spoken) is a very different experience from watching the same film on a small screen in a domestic living room with the lights on, surrounded by family members of various ages, some of whom might be shocked by the frequent swearing and references to drugs, drink and homosexuality. In this context, you might be too embarrassed to enjoy the film!

As spectators, we have different kinds of need that we might satisfy through viewing and these will affect our response. The first comment in the question suggests that one need is to maintain, or even improve upon, a sense of personal identity. This can involve being aware that there is an audience 'out there' with greater maturity, cultural experience and status, of which we are not yet a part, but to which we might aspire to belong. This can be observed even in young children. My little cousin always found most Disney films too frightening to watch, especially on her own. She would point to a copy of *Beauty and the Beast* on the shelf, saying that she knew she wouldn't like it yet. One day, when she was five, she proudly stated that since she was now a big girl, she felt able to see it (although she still wanted me to sit with her!). The film had become a sign of her growing confidence and ability to brave her fears.

Another need — suggested by the second comment in the question — might be the need for information, based on sheer curiosity about others and the world. It is interesting, even fascinating, to observe other people's reactions when we are part of an audience with them. This is especially true if they are our friends. For example, if you know people who are horror fans, a real part of the pleasure in seeing horror films with them is sharing your responses. Their screams and groans (and even laughter at the bad special effects or improbable situations) can affect your individual response as a spectator. You could watch again a cult film with which you are all familiar, such as *Braindead**, or you could introduce them to a new example. As you grow up, it becomes remarkable how different people's responses to the same film can differ. Controversial or 'shocking' films such as *Natural Born Killers** or *The Texas Chainsaw Massacre** might be seen as sick or degrading by some people (perhaps by those who have not even viewed the films themselves). Cult fans might delight in their shocking appeal. Serious film critics (or teachers!) might regard them as major works of great aesthetic or cultural significance, which you should see if you think of yourself as interested in film. Your response as an individual spectator may be affected by where you 'place' yourself along this spectrum of cultural taste.

The third comment in the question seems to suggest that we can become victims of peer pressure. Of course, laughter is infectious. However, even if we don't admit to trying to 'fit in' with the crowd, we are all, as film-goers, being constructed as members of a potential audience by the promotional and marketing hype generated by the industry (and also by the all-important 'word of mouth' and increasingly 'word of mouse' passed around by fellow film-goers and fans). We are also drawn into conversation about issues relating to a movie that might be circulating within our culture, such as rape in the case of *Baise-Moi** or the re-release of *Straw Dogs**. We may make initial genre classifications based on publicity material or our discussions with friends before we enter the auditorium, and these can determine our subsequent response to a new and unfamiliar film. They shape the emphasis we put on particular plot details, the meanings we give to various textual features, the expectations we form about likely story developments and our predictions about its resolution. After the screening we may well continue to be part of the audience in the sense that we might discuss our responses together in a variety of contexts — on the way home, or in the pub or restaurant (perhaps even one adjoining the multiplex).

People are still keen to visit cinemas to experience social interaction. There is more to cinema-going than just seeing films — there is going out at night and the sense of relaxation combined with fun and excitement. The rise of the multiplex has increased enjoyment for many, although for some the noise and crowds can make a night in watching a rented film a more attractive option.

The VCR and now the DVD player have further expanded the contexts where films might be shown. The VCR enables viewers to 'time-shift' movies so they fit more perfectly into the social dynamics of their lives. It also enables viewers to take greater control over their response to a flow of moving images, using the fast-forward function to skip past dull sections or to edit together the best bits of special effects sequences or scenes involving favourite actors.

🖉 This is a sophisticated answer, which extends the comments offered in the question in a thorough and challenging way. Contexts and modes of consumption are explored in detail and the impact of differing viewing technologies and viewing environments is explored with confidence. The candidate uses relevant examples from his or her own experience to elaborate upon and substantiate points made. This answer would be awarded 23 marks out of 25.

■ ■ ■

C-grade candidate's answer to Question 3

Not many people go to the cinema alone. It's a social event, sometimes an event before a meal. It can be planned or not, and you may not even know too much about the film you are going to see. But it's worth it to see a film on the big screen and even if the film is not very good, the excitement of the lights going down is enough.

However, at home alone, things could be different. The screen's not so big. The sofa is tempting to fall asleep on and you know that if the film gets boring, you can turn the television off. I think your surroundings can play a major part in your reactions to a film.

Annette Hill's study is a good example of why people watch films that scare or disgust them. The word gets around that there is a film you have to see because it is so scary, but would you watch it alone? You might not like it, but your friends might do. I think the quote about laughing shows that being with friends can make you feel more secure or alter your mood, so that you respond differently to a film that would otherwise make you scared. When you take a trip to the cinema your expectations are that you are going to see a good film, so perhaps you are less critical than if you were watching at home alone. However, after a cinema trip you are more likely to enter into discussion about the film with your friends and debate what you thought of it.

Sometimes people find it hard to understand a film and this is where things like DVD commentaries can be helpful. They can explain the meanings that the director and the actors see in the film and make things clearer for the viewer. Watching a film on DVD or VHS allows you to have repeat viewings, so if you don't understand something the first time around, you have a chance the second time. At the cinema, you see a film once and probably do not want to spend money seeing it again.

I think your response to a film depends on what format you watch a film in and who you are watching the film with. Peer pressure is definitely a factor when you are watching a film with friends and can affect your ability to respond as you want to. Seeing a film at the cinema is a totally different experience from seeing a film at home and people have different expectations of seeing a film on the big screen.

The candidate does attempt to discuss the impact of modes of consumption and contexts of consumption on the individual audience member. Personal experience is used fairly effectively to explain why responses to a film might be modified by DVD extras or expectations linked to the cinema-going experience. However, this response is devoid of examples, which would have made the comments more concrete. There is no attempt to use theories of consumption to explain comments or to utilise case studies of 'shocking' films to expand on points. It would be worth 14 marks out of 25.

Film and new technologies

How might DVD 'extras' and 'features' change the audience's experience of watching a film?

Total: 25 marks

■ ■ ■

A-grade candidate's answer to Question 4

There are now many more formats in which a viewer might consume a film. Film-related technology has developed to include cinema surround-sound systems, computer generated imagery, digital cameras and DVDs. The standard experience of watching a film on VHS has now been surpassed, and with DVD the viewer gains not just different information relating to a film, but a different experience of viewing.

The large storage capacity of a DVD (seven times that of a CD) allows for much more information to be included. As well as the film itself, a DVD might include trailers, production information, directorial commentaries and deleted scenes.

Therefore, via the DVD, the viewer can gain an insight into the process of the film's production. Behind-the-scenes footage and detail of how special effects are created can be accessed and give the consumer an experience of the 'mechanism' of film production. However, knowing how a particular effect has been created might be counterproductive to the experience of viewing the film itself. The 'suspension of disbelief' necessary for viewers to totally immerse themselves in the viewing experience might be affected adversely. For a student of film studies, institutional and production information is fascinating, but for the regular viewer it might explode the myth of the film being 'real'.

Directorial commentaries are a common feature of DVDs available today. The director's rationale for certain technical decisions, or their thoughts on meanings created by the film text, are available to the consumer. However, the point at which the directorial commentary is accessed within the 'viewing experience' will have an impact on the viewer's response to the film. Watched after the main feature, the commentary might encourage viewers to debate their own response in relation to the director's intent. If watched before the main feature, the preferred reading expressed by the director might influence the viewer's response and impede an independent viewing of the film.

The viewing of deleted scenes can be of great interest. The viewer can consider how the film might have looked, and the changes in narrative meaning that might have occurred, if the scenes had not been edited out. Discussion might then be prompted in the viewer as to why these scenes were omitted from the final cut. Sections from Oliver Stone's film *Natural Born Killers** that were cut in order to obtain cinematic release are included on the newly released DVD version. This can function as a marketing device, in that the extreme nature of certain deleted items might draw a consumer to purchase the 'uncut' version.

There is an interactive element to watching a film on DVD which is not possible on VHS. The DVD viewer can skip scenes easily and exit the film text to draw upon other information offered on the DVD in order to help their understanding. However, most consumers of films prefer not to have such a fragmented viewing experience.

The enhanced sound and picture quality of a DVD can certainly improve the viewer's experience, and the 'extras' on offer can make that viewer more informed about both the institutional context and potential readings of a film. However, the film itself is still the main focus of the viewing experience and the extra features included on the DVD can never make a bad film good.

⌨ This is a thorough and well-argued response, which considers the impact of DVD 'extras' in terms of the viewer's understanding of the film. The candidate has articulated some of the key debates surrounding both the marketing and the content of DVDs. Comments are explored fully and the assumption that DVD is 'better' than the technologies that it superseded is challenged. The answer shows an independent and knowledgeable response to the question and would be worth 24 out of 25 marks.

■ ■ ■

C-grade candidate's answer to Question 4

Most shops now sell films on DVD, and VHS has become almost obsolete. You can still buy VHS videos, but they are often in sales, implying that the technology is being pushed out by DVD.

DVDs have many 'extras' and 'features' that can affect the way in which they are viewed. The consumer today can watch extra scenes from a film, listen to interviews with actors or the director, and look at all the trailers attached to the film.

DVDs have improved sound and pictures, which will make the viewer's experience better, because the film will seem more dramatic and exciting. A DVD might include a widescreen option, which will allow the viewer to feel as if they are in the cinema and not just in their living room. The chapter index on DVDs is useful, as it allows the viewer to go to the scene they want to view, rather than having to fast-forward or rewind, which they would have to do if watching a VHS copy of the film.

Listening to what the actors or the director say about the film is also useful, as the viewer can get more information about what scenes or action sequences might mean. Extra scenes are interesting to the viewer of the film, as they might add information. For example, the deleted 'spider walk' scene included on the DVD of *The Exorcist** showed Regan's possession and was really frightening.

The trailers included on a DVD can give the viewer information about how the film was marketed and which elements of the film were focused on in the advertising. Viewers can also compare their expectations, based on watching the trailer, to their experience of watching the actual film.

Overall, DVDs allow viewers to have a much better experience of watching a film. They give fascinating information and plenty of opportunity for the viewers to increase their understanding of what they are watching.

✍ This is a solid answer that identifies the main differences between DVD and VHS and discusses in some detail the impact of 'extras' and 'features' on the viewer. The candidate has included his or her own experience of DVD viewing usefully and has considered the issue of an altered viewing experience quite effectively. However, the answer does not challenge DVD viewing and discusses all DVD 'extras' and 'features' positively. A greater acknowledgement of the interaction between the viewer and the DVD would have improved the candidate's score of 15 marks out of 25.